STREETCARS

&

OTHER VEHICLES

stories by

Ronald Sparling

First published by Third Wheel Publishing

Kelowna, Canada
thirdwheelpublishing@gmail.com
thirdwheelpublishi.wixsite.com/books

This book is a work of fiction. Names, characters, places and incidences either are products of the author's imagination or are used fictitiously. Any resemblance to events or locales or persons, living or dead, is entirely coincidental.

ISBN-13: 978-0-9952861-1-5 (print edition)

ISBN – 10: 0995286116 (print edition)

This book is dedicated to, Martha Maier, whose support and editing are invaluable.

What Clara Knew and *Holes* first appeared in The Dalhousie Review.

Streetcars and Other Vehicles first appeared in The Antigonish Review.

All the Useless Things, *The Diner*, and *Legs* first appeared in PIF Magazine.

ronsparling@gmail.com
ronaldsparling.wixsite.com/freelance
facebook.com/ronald.sparling.5
https://twitter.com/RonaldSparling

Contents

Legs

It went something like this:

> Dear Ann: I recently married a mortician. Although I had previously participated in heavy petting, technically, I was still a virgin. On our wedding night my husband told me to soak in a cold bath until my body was frigid. He then instructed me to lie on the bed without moving while he made love to me. Is this normal? If not, what should I do?

Get out of the house, Ann told her. Immediately. And call the police.

Maybe Ann should have told her to get used to it.

Maybe I'm just bitter.

****

I dropped in on Grant one morning last week - unexpectedly. I should have known by his face when he saw me, by the way his eyes darted back into the house, by the way he hesitated before stepping aside to allow me to enter.

She walked out of the bathroom, one towel wrapped around her body, using another to dry her long, blond hair. She hesitated only a split second before a smile cracked her plastic-clear skin. You must be Sarah, she said. I'm Angela. I live upstairs.

No response.

Oh, she said. I know this looks bad, but it really isn't. My own shower's broken, and Grant was kind enough to offer me his.

I swung toward Grant. He held out his hands as if to say - See. No weapon. Her shower's broken, he said, and then smiled nervously.

Angela emitted an awkward laugh. I've got to get to work, she said, and disappeared into Grant's bedroom.

I gaped at Grant in disbelief, but he just shrugged, turned away and busied himself with pouring coffee. Her shower was broken, he repeated. What was I supposed to do? Don't start making a big deal about it, Sarah. Nothing happened.

I was still standing in the middle of the kitchen staring at Grant, who was half leaning against the counter playing with his coffee, when Angela returned in tight jeans and a white tank top that screamed, "I don't need a bra."

She thanked Grant and gave me a quick, cruel smile as she manoeuvred her way out the door.

Without a word I walked into Grant's bedroom. The unmistakable smell of sex hung in the air like a mushroom cloud. I suppose I should have been more understanding; it had been at least thirty-six hours since we'd made love.

I walked back out to the kitchen where Grant was now seated at the table, reading the paper, trying to look nonchalant. So? he asked. What are you doing here at this hour? I wasn't expecting you.

Obviously not.

Jesus, Sarah, he said. It's no big deal. She lives upstairs. He spoke as if that made it all right.

Is this why you wanted me to wear a blond wig? So you could fuck me and pretend I was Angela?

The wig has nothing to do with Angela. The only reason the wig would turn me on is because you'd be the one wearing it.

What a crock.

As soon as Grant realized I wasn't going to believe "nothing" happened, he changed tactics, tried his biological-determination theory on me. Men are different from women, he explained. Women are monogamous by nature. Men need variety. It has something to do with the hormones we get as foetuses, he said, but it has nothing to do with us, nothing to do with you and me.

Bullshit. Even Ann Landers would know that.

****

Grant phoned me at the studio that afternoon. Said he wanted a chance to explain. I told him there was nothing to explain, that he already had. It's in our genes, I said. I'm just a woman. I want someone who won't fuck other people. Then I hung up.

****

I phoned Monica to see if she wanted to play squash, maybe go for a drink afterward. She said she could do the squash, but she couldn't drink. She's pregnant - again.

This is the third time. She has the cutest kids. They hardly ever spit up on you.

I took care of them for a weekend once, so she and Dan could get away. It was great fun, up to my elbows in diapers and vaseline. Cured me from ever wanting my own.

So why do I need someone like Grant in my life?

Sex?

He was good in bed.

Every move was calculated. He never came before I did.

****

Grant phoned again, later that afternoon, to ask about our tickets to a play the following night. I'd totally forgotten. I told him to take Angela, unless he was already tired of her.

Damn. I really wanted to see that play.

****

Monica says I'm in a rut. Says I pick the same type of guy every time. That's why I end up getting hurt. Not because there are no good men out there. Look at Dan, she says.

I don't have the heart to tell her Dan made a pass at me once - in their kitchen.

We were drunk so it didn't really count. Later, he acted as though it had never happened.

Maybe it hadn't.

Maybe I just imagined the whole thing because I wanted him to.

And maybe I am in a rut. Maybe what I need is a nice accountant who wants to replace his mother. Clean the dishes. Clean the house. Make the meals. Spend the week making a job list so he'll have something to do on weekends.

So we will have something to discuss at the dinner table.

I really need a new kitchen, dear. How else can I keep making these wonderful meals?

Just get me a goddamn microwave for our Lean Cuisine and I'll never ask for another thing.

Of course, I'm joking. Cooking is my life.

****

Grant phoned again the next day, to offer me the tickets. I said no.

I'm only trying to do the right thing, he said.

He's only trying to play the martyr. This way, when he's explaining our break-up to his friends, he can nod his head with sacrificial nobility and say: Naturally, I let her have the theatre tickets.

****

Yesterday, I went to Grant's apartment, to pick up things I'd left there. He walked around moodily, followed me from room to room, kept asking why I thought this was necessary. Couldn't we just talk, try to work things out.

Then the phone rang. I knew by his voice and the look of panic he shot in my direction that it was Angela. I was out the door before he could hang up, my arms full. I walked around to the back of his building and threw it all in the green dumpster.

****

There was a message on my machine from Grant when I got home. He said I've blown things way out of proportion. He asked me to call him when I've calmed down.

There was also a message from Monica inviting me for dinner. Her voice sounded sad and worried. I think she's taking this harder than I am. She has a new book for me. Something about why women pick the men they do. She said it will help me out of my rut.

I didn't return her call. I have enough to think about without worrying about her worrying about me.

****

There was a time, not that long ago, when all of my friends were giving me self-help books. I hadn't realized I was in such a pitiful state. One book tried to convince me that I need not be depressed about my present situation, even though all of my friends are married and starting families. My time would come, it assured me. For now, I was to rejoice in my independence and take full advantage of the freedom it afforded me.

My favourite self-help book was given to me by Kasha. Kasha's on her third marriage, drives a Porsche and has a seemingly endless stream of lovers. She has what she calls a healthy disdain for men and is deliriously happy.

The book she gave me insisted that life was not worth living without a good partner. It provided ten easy-to-follow rules on how to find this perfect mate. I could never get past the first rule: always be happy. It reminded me of a town of zombie-wives in an old movie I'd once seen. I think it starred Catherine Ross. The real wives had been replaced by cheerful, mindless androids; a town full of June Cleavers without opinions or passion. But, God, the men were happy!

****

Dear Ann: My husband wants me to be happy all of the time. No matter how hard I try, I just can't seem to get it right. I keep letting little things like global warming, ethnic cleansing, and his infidelity bother me. What can I do? - Tired of Thinking

Dear Tired of Thinking: Stop thinking. If that doesn't work, try warm milk and valium.

****

My mother must have read Ann Landers. Only instead of warm milk she used vodka. Suicide at a snail's pace.

****

Dinner at Mom and Dad's. My two brothers sitting opposite me, on the boys' side, me alone on the girls'. Mom apologizing for the food that lay on our plates like a burnt offering while she swills down her wine like it's the blood of Christ.

From the other end of the table my father booms out his jokes.

How do you cure a woman of nymphomania?

My brothers watch him expectantly, even though they've heard the joke a hundred times.

Marry her!

Mom scolds him good-naturedly, hides a smile behind her glass.

I try to ignore him.

Why's a woman's thing so close to her ass?

So you can pick her up like a six pack and carry her home!

My mother titters surreptitiously. Oh, Harold. That's terrible.

That's disgusting, I tell him, but he simply looks at me with pity that I'm not a boy and, therefore, cannot be expected to understand.

My brothers slap each other on the back and say: Good one, Dad!

****

After deciding not to return Monica's call I returned to my studio, smoked a joint and uncovered my canvas. Large, black eyes loomed out from a pale, emancipated body. The figure had long fingernails that curled like a series of pig cocks (I had once been told that a pig's penis was actually turned like a corkscrew and have never been able to shake the image). In the figure's hands, which were extended toward me, lay a small, bloodied object, like a freshly slaughtered religious sacrifice. It wasn't clear what the object was, but I knew.

Time to re-evaluate my outlook on life, I thought, as I picked up a brush and prepared to paint over it.

****

Dinner at Mom and Dad's. Mom apologizes for nuking the food too long. She destroyed two microwaves before my father finally threw out all of her metal cooking sheets.

As if she ever cooks a damn thing anymore, he said.

My brothers have moved out west where they own a paving company. Before I got married they would phone me at three in the morning, drunk, to see if I was getting any.

We worry about our little sis, one would always say.

Don't use it and it'll dry up, the other would always add. Then they'd laugh and say in unison: Good one, Bro.

Since they've moved out west they don't use each other's names anymore.

In my brothers' place sits Peter, my first and only husband. He laughs politely at Dad's jokes, and even tells some of his own, but they are political, and I know my father is disappointed in my choice.

So, it turned out, was Peter.

****

I want children, Peter said. You want to paint. They just don't go together, do they?

I shrugged. Tears ran down my cheeks. I knew he was right.

Can't you just be a big brother?

****

Instead of painting over the bloody blob that lay in the hands, I frantically added more blood, until it dripped down the figure's gown and formed a pool of dark red on the ground beneath its feet. I knew if I stopped to think about what I was doing, it would never get done.

Behind the figure I painted a large building with flames licking up the sides.

I was almost certain who lay sleeping in the building.

****

Dinner at Mom and Dad's. Mom does not apologize for the food. We've ordered in Chinese. My father tries to tell his jokes, but Mom no longer listens, and he knows they're wasted on me.

Mom's filling her glass and telling me I must have done something to drive Peter away.

We just wanted different things, I said.

Well, Dear. You must have done something. Men are different from women. They have different needs and desires. You've just got to realize that and accept it.

My father clears his throat and rises from the table to watch a ball game.

****

My father left my mother for the secretary in his construction office four months ago. Not long afterward, the telephone calls began: my mother threatening to kill herself. She would phone and I would rush over to her house, no matter what time it was. In the morning she rarely remembered calling me and would ask what I was doing sleeping on the couch.

Last night she forgot to call.

The funeral is postponed for longer than usual so it can be held on Saturday. This is for my brothers' benefit.

****

Looking at my mother in her casket, I realize for the first time what a large woman she was. I'd always pictured her to be so tiny that I'm shocked to find I could have been so wrong.

After the funeral, after my mother's exaggerated body has been placed in the ground, we return to her house to greet bereaved relatives and guests. When they finally leave, we sit down at my mother's table and eat as we had as children, except in my mother's place sits Charlene, my father's new love.

It doesn't take long for my father to begin with his jokes. Trying to lighten the mood I suppose. I shouldn't really blame him. He hasn't seen his sons for several years.

Peter was at the funeral, and although my father invited him to stay for the meal, and I assured him he was welcome, he declined pleading other commitments. I already knew about his other commitments and didn't mind in the least. Perhaps she did.

Grant was nowhere to be seen. He may not have even known.

****

Dinner at Mom and Dad's. Mom is no longer there. Charlene, her recently de-greyed, jet-black hair, tied back into a pony tail that I think looks ridiculous on a woman her age, is going on about how nice my mother must have been for so many people to have gone through so much trouble to prepare such nice food for the family.

My father is telling one of his jokes. Why does a woman have legs?

From nowhere the answers begin pouring out of my mouth.

So she can run away from a husband who's fucking his secretary.

So she can kick a man in the crotch when he comes at her with a knife.

So she can ...

I stop and look up at the astonished faces that stare, open-mouthed, in my direction.

But then my father clears his throat. That ... that's not it at all, he says. It's so she doesn't leave sludge marks like a snail.

Suddenly, the real answer carves its way into my head, and I feel it snake down my neck, slither forward toward my mouth where it exits in a barely audible whisper.

So she can walk from the ice-cold bath to the bed.

What Clara Knew

"Mr. Feller has disappeared"

Clara Humphries, widow of the late Corporal Lloyd Humphries, as she informed everyone she met, made her announcement with grim satisfaction - satisfaction because she had news, grim because she did not know the whole story - yet.

Her daughter, Elizabeth, continued ironing as Clara steered her electric wheelchair through the doorway of the small, second-floor apartment she shared with Elizabeth and Elizabeth's seven-year-old daughter, Jessica. Not actually confined to the wheelchair, it provided Clara with the mobility she would have otherwise lacked. She tired so easily these days. By coincidence, the missing Mr. Feller had the exact same model, except different, as Clara had explained to Elizabeth.

"What do you mean, disappeared?"

"I mean just that. Disappeared. Gone. He wasn't in our spot yesterday, and he wasn't there again today."

For the past several months Clara and Mr. Feller had parked their chairs across from each other on either side of the square separating their buildings. Although they had never actually spoken, Clara was certain they knew all about each other, or at least Clara felt she knew all that was needed about Mr. Feller.

"Did you ever think maybe he just stayed in his apartment, watching a movie or something? Maybe he needs the rest. He's awfully old."

Clara had to agree. Mr. Feller was at least five years older than she. But still, he was not in his spot and no one knew why. Actually, Clara hadn't yet had the time or the courage to ask anyone.

Clara acquired most of her information concerning Mr. Feller through Millie Tate, who lived on the fourth floor of their building, and whose son played with Mr. Feller's grandson. Millie was an acquaintance of Elizabeth's. Clara would not exactly call them friends as Millie had yet to include Clara in an invitation for dinner. Millie felt grandmothers were only for baby-sitting. Not that Clara minded. But once in a while it would have been nice to go out, even if Millie's apartment was just upstairs.

In addition, Millie was not the sort Clara wished her daughter to be too close to. She was rather forward and laughed too easily to be proper. Clara was certain Millie must have been a wild child. Perhaps even a bit loose, although Clara would never actually voice that opinion.

Be that as it may, through Millie, Clara knew that Mr. Feller was a recent widower - it had been less than ten years since the death of his wife. She knew he lived with his daughter, her husband, and their two sons in a three-bedroom unit in the same subsidised housing development as Clara. She also knew they paid about six hundred dollars in rent, an amount she thought enormously unfair to Elizabeth, whose own two-bedroom apartment was almost as much.

But aside from the information obtained from Millie, Clara thought she knew a great deal more about Mr. Feller. Sitting each day in the same park, literally yards apart, Clara had developed a relationship between them, a relationship based on the silent bond created by their common situations and by the fence surrounding their park.

She was certain Mr. Feller shared many of her feelings about the world around them. Her dismay at the price of things. Her shock with the apparent immorality of the day's young people. Her fear of the growing violence. And Clara felt that Mr. Feller was as fond of his grandchildren as she was of Jessica.

If they had talked, Clara imagined their conversations would have been full of interesting titbits about their married lives and how both their spouses - may they rest in peace - would be happy for them to have companionship. Clara, however, felt that proper respect for the dead would not allow their relationship to develop past friendship, no matter what Mr. Feller's intentions.

Clara always blushed at this thought, and, her embarrassment increasing, she was certain Mr. Feller would raise his head from the books he constantly read, notice her red face and immediately know the cause. Thus, Clara rarely allowed herself to entertain those thoughts. She had censored them with her Lloyd and she certainly wasn't going to allow them to flourish around another.

And she had censored them with her Lloyd. Lying still and quiet as his body moved gently over her own. Unable to respond to his whispers of love, not because she didn't want to, but because she dared not open her mouth. Could she trust only words to come out? And what if Lloyd knew? Would he think her a wanton woman?

He asked her once, before they got married, "Do you love me?" and she hesitated, out of shyness, not for the reasons he assumed as he turned away. "You will," he said. "In time, you will."

By the time Lloyd was lying in bed, grey ashen skin the colour of driftwood draped over brittle bones, eyes like a trapped bird's, frightened and frantic, it was too late. She couldn't tell him the way she felt. Her Lloyd was gone. And she didn't recognise the withered cast-off he'd left behind. Didn't know how to calm those frightened eyes.

Each afternoon Clara returned to her apartment and reported to Elizabeth what was new in the world of Mr. Feller, as she understood it. For instance, she knew his whole wardrobe, or at least the out-of-doors portion, and from this deciphered his birthday. Mr. Feller had arrived in a brand new sweater on the eleventh of April. But, to be honest, Clara was unsure if his birthday was on the tenth or the eleventh. It really depended on whether his family celebrated birthdays in the morning or at dinner time. They appeared to Clara to be a morning family.

But frequently, what Clara had to report was the product of speculation rather than of fact: Clara was not the sort to let facts get in the way of knowing the truth. More often than not she based her speculation on the reading Mr. Feller did each afternoon. "You can't tell a book by its cover," Clara would tell her daughter, "but you can tell a person by their book."

She deduced his interest in prehistoric times from his reading of Life Before Man. And she told Elizabeth of the trouble Mr. Feller's daughter was having with her husband when he made his way through A Maggot.

After discovering him with a copy of Hard Times, she informed Elizabeth that the recent recession had not left Mr. Feller unscathed. She worried until she saw Big Money held high before him, which set her mind somewhat at ease and she silently wished him luck.

Clara was especially affected when she had to suffer through Mr. Feller's reading of In the Heat of the Night. For several days she found she was blushing more often than she deemed proper.

But Clara was particularly upset by the last few books Mr. Feller read immediately before his disappearance. She felt that he had lost faith in the Lord and was preparing for death in a new and unholy fashion. It began with a book entitled Of Good and Evil. Clara attempted to dismiss it as an exploration for interest's sake, but Heart of Darkness followed, which lead directly to the final book before his vanishing, The Rebel Angels.

That, Clara told her daughter, was a perfect example of why she never read anything but the Bible. Mr. Feller was almost certainly a God-fearing man before his mind was swayed by words unfit for human consumption. She knew he was a believer because some time ago she had seen him reading The Papers of Samuel Middlemarch, and if Samuel Middlemarch was not the name of a man of the cloth, then Clara didn't know what was.

And now Mr. Feller was gone - vanished - without a word or a trace, and Clara was worried for his soul.

As usual, her daughter did not share Clara's fears, but she agreed to ask Millie what she knew when she came down for her nightly visit, visits Clara suspected Millie used as a means of escaping her husband and children.

"But I wish you'd use your time a little more constructively," Elizabeth said. "Have you cleaned your room like I asked?"

With nothing to do but wait for Millie's arrival, and wanting to ensure her daughter's sympathies, Clara set about cleaning.

By the time Millie arrived, Elizabeth had completely forgotten her mother's concerns, although Clara had purposely mentioned Mr. Feller several more times. So Clara took it upon herself to casually inquire whether Millie had heard anything new about Mr. Feller.

"Still got the hots for him, eh, Clara?" Millie was forever accusing Clara of harbouring a secret desire for Mr. Feller, another reason Clara would not call Millie and Elizabeth friends.

Clara tried to feign indifference and told Millie to stop her foolishness. "I'm merely concerned for his welfare. He hasn't been outside for the past couple of days." Clara could feel the blood rising to her face.

"Don't you go worrying about that, Clara. If something had happened, I'd have heard by now. You wait and see. Your lovebird'll be back tomorrow. Maybe you'll even get meet him."

Clara turned away, offended by Millie's disrespectful allusion to

Mr. Feller and the laughter her last comment had caused, but she did hope Millie was right.

That night Clara could hardly sleep. What if something had indeed happened to her Mr. Feller. They would never have the chance to meet. She would never have the chance to tell him how she felt about ...

... about what? About him? That was ridiculous. She didn't even know him.

That would have to change. Decision made. If Mr. Feller showed up the next day, Clara was going to march right up and introduce herself. She had every right to. It was only proper. Wasn't it, in fact, strange that Mr. Feller had not yet done so himself?

Yes. Clara would make the first move, but she didn't mention her decision to anyone, just in case.

The following morning Elizabeth greeted Clara with the news of Mr. Feller's illness. "Millie said it looks serious. You want eggs this morning?"

Clara slumped into a kitchen chair, her elbows landing heavily on the tabletop.

"I'm going to see him."

"Going to see who?"

"Mr. Feller. I'm going to visit Mr. Feller."

"Oh, Mom. You don't even know him. What will you say?"

"I don't know."

****

In the slit of sunlight between the drawn curtains, Clara could see dust particles floating. Dead skin, she thought. Discarded grey and useless.

The woman was gently touching Mr. Feller's arm. "Dad. Dad.

This is Mrs. Humphries. She's come to say her respects. To say hello. Dad?"

To say goodbye, Clara thought.

Mr. Feller's eyes flickered but remained shut. "I'm afraid he's not very with it. Would you like to sit for a minute? I can open the drapes a bit."

"No. I mean yes, but please, leave the drapes."

Clara looked about the room. It was a boy's room. Posters of hockey players. A model plane hanging above the bureau. Nothing to suggest a grown man lived here. When the kids let you move in, they didn't allow you to bring much. They knew it was temporary. And why should they have to deal with your garbage when you're gone?

When Clara looked back, Mr. Feller was watching her. She couldn't tell if he recognised her, but she recognised the frightened, pleading eyes. Had seen them before.

She reached out and took his hand. It trembled, then suddenly clamped tightly down upon her own. Startled by his strength, Clara almost withdrew her hand. Then she returned the pressure.

Mr. Feller's eyes softened, then closed, leaving Clara seated in the dark, his hand in hers as she listened to the soft rasping of his aged breath.

I like you so much

"I like you so much," she said. "I wish you lived in another city. Then we could see each other only on weekends and I could miss you terribly all week. We could feel this way about each other forever. Every time we saw each other it would be special."

"Maybe we could just avoid each other during the week," he said.

"Could we? Would you do that for me."

He nodded.

"But we can't ever fall in love," she added. "I want to go away and I don't want to miss anyone when I do."

After she did leave, he enjoyed his wretchedness immensely, reading poetry and listening to Tom Waits and writing to her constantly telling her how miserable he was without her. And for the next few weeks, he wrote a great deal of what he felt was his best work to date.

That spring she was deported from Mexico for leaving her teaching post. When she entered the bar she paused at his table and said hello. He simply mumbled a reply and did not turn around to look at her the rest of the evening, but drank his beer and tried instead to listen to his friends. At one point he thought of walking over and smiling as he poured a beer over her head, but not because he cared, but because she should have.

"I don't know how you do it," one of his friends said. "After all those letters you wrote."

A few days later when he heard she'd left town and gone to Toronto because she was afraid he might call, his faced burned with indignation. How could she not know he'd already gotten all he could from her?

Freddie

William would never call Dennis a bastard to his face. Even at twelve, he knew you couldn't make fun of people for things that are real, unless you wanted to hurt them. But the fact remained, his cousin was a bastard and in more ways than one. Born to William's Aunt Alice, his mother's youngest sister, Dennis had no real father. William's mother once told him that Dennis's father had died of a sinus infection before he was able to marry Alice, and although William pretended to believe her, the fact was he didn't. Whoever heard of someone dying from a runny nose? William thought his mother should have been able to come up with a better story than that.

Dennis's mother married a man who owned his own plumbing company while Dennis was still a baby, and they were now referred to by their cousins as the rich relatives. Christmas at his cousin's house in the city was always a sought after treat. Dennis and his sister got more toys than you could shake a stick at. That's what William's father said, more toys than you could shake a stick at. William was never jealous, though. He was just happy to have the chance to play with them while they were still new. Toys never lasted long around Dennis.

William's mother mentioned several times a summer how lucky her sister had been. How lucky she was to have been born with looks. And how generous her brother-in-law, William's uncle Charlie, had been to have taken in a woman and her illegitimate son. "Things were different back then," she would say. "An unmarried mother was not as commonplace as it is today. Not as sociably acceptable. If you could have seen the expression on Charlie's mother's face at the wedding. She was fit to be tied." William imagined Charlie's mother roped to a pew to keep from halting the ceremony. To keep from beating on his Aunt Alice.

Each afternoon William and Dennis walked down the lane that ran between their two families' properties and lead from the lake to the main road. They walked down the lane and crossed the road to buy candy at Miriam's Groceries and Bait Shop. William's mother only gave him a nickel or a dime, but Dennis seemed to have an unlimited supply of cash. William wasn't keen on these trips, but it got so they were expected, and to have refused would have meant explaining, and that was something William couldn't do. But the fact was, Dennis was not only a bastard, he was a thief.

Miriam was an old woman, could hardly have run the place by herself, but she had her son, Ed, to help her out. Ed was pretty old too, maybe even in his thirties, but he stayed and ran the store with his mother because he wasn't right in the head. William felt sorry for Ed but Dennis made a game of tormenting him. Walked around the store looking as suspicious as he could so that Ed would know he was going to steal something and try and keep his eye on him but he couldn't all the time, especially if there were other people there.

On days when there were no other people, Dennis sent William up to the cash register to pay for their candy bars and then on the way home he'd pull stuff out of his pockets and show William everything he'd stolen. "Ed's so stupid," he'd say.

Even though William hated being a part of it, he said nothing about how he felt. About how he didn't want to be a part of stealing from anyone, especially from someone who wasn't even right in the head. It just didn't seem fair. But he said nothing because he knew Dennis would only laugh at him and call him a little kid.

Dennis was only two years older than William, but William

knew that in the city Dennis would have had nothing to do with him. At the cottage, it was different. At the cottage you hung out with whomever was available. William supposed his parents liked that, liked that the families got together, that he got to know his cousins. He could hardly tell them Dennis was a bastard, or what his mother would have called a bad influence.

****

The boys sat on the ridge that overlooked their cottages and the lake and ate what they'd brought from the store. Dennis handed William some of the candy from his pocket.

"No thanks," William said.

"Don't be stupid. I got it for both of us."

William knew that was a lie. Dennis had stolen it all for himself, but knew that if he could get William to take some, that made him an accomplice. It meant William couldn't tell anyone.

"Look," Dennis said. "I got those strawberry things you like so much. Don't tell me I risked everything for you and you don't even want it."

William took the candies from his hand and placed them on the ground beside him.

"Aren't you going to try one?"

"Maybe."

"Go on, have one. Of course, if you don't want them, I'm sure I can find someone to hang out with that does."

William popped one in his mouth.

"Well?"

"Thanks," William said.

When William had been sick a couple of weeks previously, Dennis visited each day with a pocket full of candy and they sat on the floor in the living room and ate. Afterwards, when William was able to go back up to the store with him, Dennis asked him for money. He figured out that at a chocolate bar a day, William owed him somewhere in the neighbourhood of two dollars, but he was willing to take one. Because they were cousins. William knew his aunt had probably given Dennis extra money to buy something for him, but gave him the money anyway.

After eating their candy, the boys walked along the path that led through the trees to the old Decker place. Old man Decker never came up anymore, not since his wife died and his children moved away. The cottage stood high on a hill and was surrounded by crab apple trees. They weren't any good for eating but made for great apple fights. Dennis always won because he wasn't afraid to throw them as hard as he could, something William would never dream of doing. Afterward, William's mother would ask where the bruises came from and William would tell her he'd fallen in the woods. He knew she didn't really believe him, it happened too often, but after a moment or two of silence when William was sure she was studying him but wouldn't raise his eyes to see, she'd tell him to be more careful and go on to something else.

In amongst the trees, the boys found an old shopping cart, abandoned on its side, and took turns pushing each other around. Every time William was inside, it tipped over or crashed into a tree. William didn't push it fast enough for Dennis's liking, so they bored of it quickly.

"I got an idea," Dennis said, heading down the path towards home pushing the cart ahead of him. When they weren't far from the house Dennis told William to call Freddie. Freddie was a small black lab who had adopted William's family for the summer. He lived on a farm a couple of miles down the road, but spent most of his time hanging out on their back porch. William had gone with his father to talk to the farmer who'd said he didn't give a damn if the dog ever came back.

Freddie came bounding out and Dennis placed him in the cart.

William wanted to know what he was going to do.

"Push him down the hill into the water."

William protested but Dennis explained how dogs were always wanting to prove their loyalty to their masters and that this was one way Freddie could do it. He wouldn't mind, Dennis said. "In fact, it'll probably be fun for him."

At first they started from not far up the hill, but each time Dennis dragged the cart a little higher until they no longer had to push and the cart went hurtling down the hill on its own, Freddie seated shivering inside. He looked at William with big, sad brown eyes each time Dennis hoisted him in. William looked away. Afterward, they pulled the cart out of the water and the dog would shake himself off and then Dennis would feel his legs and check for broken bones as if he knew what he was doing. As if the whole exercise was a science experiment.

Finally, William could take it no longer and when Freddie came out of the water, he tried to chase him away yelling and waving his arms. But the dog simply cowered on the ground looking submissive and confused. William fell beside him and wrapped his arms around the dog's neck.

"You're not going to do it anymore."

Dennis stood over him. "Who's going to stop me?"

With that William leapt to his feet and swung out with his fist at Dennis's face. Dennis side-stepped the blow easily and punched hard into William's stomach, sending him sprawling on the ground gasping for air.

"You bastard," William managed to say.

Dennis laughed. "You're such a little gear box," which was what he called queers, then he walked away. William didn't really know what queers were, but he knew his cousin hated them.

****

"If you're not a gearbox," Dennis said, "you'll kiss her." He had William pinned beneath him. Beneath William was Debbie, Dennis's cousin from across the bay. Debbie was Dennis's age and wasn't really William's cousin because she was related to Dennis on the other side of his family. On his father's side. She, too, was laughing which didn't surprise William because Dennis was always telling him she was a slut. He claimed to have felt her up, but William didn't believe him. Dennis lied at will. He lied even when it wasn't for any reason, just because he felt like it.

But here she was, pressed beneath William and he could feel the smoothness of her skin because they were in bathing suits and every time he squirmed her felt her breasts move. They were large for her age because she was pleasingly plump, as his mother said.

She was laughing and saying, "Come on, William. One little kiss won't hurt you." And then she rolled over so that Dennis fell off and she was on top pinning William's arms above his head. William struggled, but he was no match for her. She lowered her head and he tried to twist away but then her lips were against his and he was kissing her and Donnie was laughing.

"Lookit here. He's got a boner."

Debbie looked behind her. "Oh God, he does!" she squealed. "Let's see it." She swung her legs around so she sat above William's head and her legs pinned his arms, while Dennis caught hold of his flailing legs and sat on them. In one swift motion, he yanked William's suit down.

William ceased his struggling. He looked down at his little penis as it bobbed in the air and then shrank in embarrassment. He could hear Debbie squealing that it was such a cute little thing. And Dennis laughing at his baldness. And then he heard no more. The tears were streaming silently from beneath the eyelids he'd scrunched closed. And the blood pounded in his ears like an African drum. He felt the pressure leave his arms and his legs and he rolled over and tucked his legs into his stomach and tried to stem the flow of tears but they wouldn't stop. And he stayed that way, with his eyes closed, until the blood stopped beating in his ears and he heard Debbie and Dennis move off still laughing and knew he was alone.

****

The night had been set aside for the adults. Everyone ate at one house, at Dennis's, and then the kids were sent away. William and Dennis were to spend the evening at William's cottage.

When they arrived the cottage was dark. Dennis wanted to leave it that way, but William ran around and turned on most of the lights. The front half of the cottage, the kitchen, dining room and living room, was all open. The back half was divided into three bedrooms and a washroom. Dennis walked around the living room flipping through magazines and touching everything while William watched him worried. He knew his cousin was not going to make the night easy. Finally, Dennis stopped and opened the doors to the liquor cabinet.

He whistled softly. "Now that's what I call entertainment," he said, examining the bottles one by one and placing them on the floor.

"Put them away."

"Shut up. I'm just looking at them. And if I did decide to have some, it's not like your parents could ever tell. See. I could just take a sip of this one." He opened a bottle and lifted it to his mouth. Screwed the top back on and grabbed another bottle. "And then a sip of this one."

"You better stop that."

"Why?"

"Because they could come home any time now. I heard my parents say they weren't going to stay late."

"That's bullshit. They're doing the same thing at my place right now." Dennis opened another bottle and held it up to the light. "Crown Royal," he said. "Now this is good stuff."

He took a drink, then stood and walked around the room, the bottle dangling loose and dangerous in his hand. Swaggered in his best adult style. Suddenly, he stopped dead in his tracks. Turned his head slowly and looked at William. "Where are your mom's cigarettes?"

"No way."

"Just tell me where they are, and I won't have to kill you." He saw William's glance and bounded toward the drawers in the kitchen. Yanked them open one by one until he raised a pack high before him. "Thank you, Lord. The final touch." He plopped down on the couch, grabbed the lighter off the coffee table and lighted one. He held it like a cigar and blew the smoke out slowly savouring every molecule. Then he rinsed his mouth with the whiskey. "Young master William. You really must try this."

"Not me. When they find out, they're going to kill you."

"You're almost a teenager now, aren't you? Well, part of being a teenager is doing things your parents tell you not to. And if they find out, which they won't unless you tell them, they won't kill us. It's what they expect us to do. We're teenagers. We listen to the Beatles, for Christ's sake. Now get you little ass over here and try some of this before I have to make you."

William sat on the floor across from Dennis. He took the bottle. Felt the liquid burn on his lips and pulled the bottle away.

"Oh, for crying out loud. Take a drink."

This time William took a large gulp. His throat burned. He gasped for air, sputtering, while his cousin fetched a glass of water.

"Not so much this time. Take it slow," Dennis said.

William took a deep breath. His task was clear. He must drink the whiskey without gagging. He raised the bottle to his lips and threw his head back so that a mouthful flooded in and then jerked the bottle back down. He swallowed some, held the rest in his mouth as long as he could, and swallowed again.

"Now that's the way to do it. Here. Give it back. Want some of this?"

William grabbed the cigarette and took a small drag. Blew it out. "Nothing to it," he said.

"Try inhaling, gearbox."

The smoke halted halfway through its descent toward his lungs, and for a second, William couldn't breathe. Then the muscles of his throat relaxed and the smoke was in. It came out in a flurry of coughing. He grabbed at the water.

"Forget that. Have some more rye."

William reached for the bottle.

****

William lifted his head from the floor. Dennis was nowhere to be seen. The house was quiet. The bottle still stood on the table, along with the cigarettes. Ashes were spread about the half-full ashtray. It seemed to him the middle of the night. He pulled himself up using the coffee table for support and shuffled to the kitchen. The clock read less than nine fifteen. His head hurt and he was groggy and trying to figure out what had happened. What was going on. He saw a light from the under the bathroom door and walked toward it. He opened the door.

Dennis was seated on the toilet. Spread open on the floor about him were William's mother's magazines. Redbook and Chatelaine. He held another folded open across one thigh. His other hand was pumping in and out between his legs.

It took only a few seconds for the scene to penetrate the haze that fogged William's mind. About the same amount of time it took Dennis to notice him standing in the door.

Dennis's face burned an instant red. "Get out!" he screamed. "Get the fuck out!"

William slammed the door shut.

He was replacing the bottles in the cabinet when Dennis came out. "Don't you know how to knock, you little gear box?"

"I didn't know where you were."

"I wasn't doing anything. I was just reading." Dennis looked nervous. Looked angry.

"I didn't say anything."

"Well, you better not, either. Don't forget, I know what you did tonight."

It didn't seem to dawn on Dennis that he'd been doing the same things, but William decided against pointing this out. "We need to clean up."

Dennis flopped onto the couch. "You do it," he said. "I'm tired."

William carried the ashtray to the kitchen, dumped the butts into the garbage beneath the sink and rinsed it. "I think you should go," he said.

"What?"

"You heard me. I want you to go home."

"You must be kidding."

"I want you to leave." William had stopped cleaning.

"I'm not going anywhere." William made no reply. "Fine, I'm out of here. Who wants to hang out with a little gear box like you anyway."

William sat on the counter and listened. Faint voices drifted across the lawn from the other cottage. A toilet flushed. Water ran in a sink. He watched his cousin's shadow cross the path of light that sliced from the side door across the lawn. Heard Dennis's footsteps on the far porch and the outside door open and close. Voices inside rose in surprise.

William knew someone would be over soon. Probably his parents. They wouldn't leave him there by himself, even if they were only a few dozen yards away. And if not his parents, someone would come.

He climbed down off the counter and went to his room. Took off his clothes and climbed between the sheets of his bed.

William felt strange. Like something was different. Like he was different. It wasn't the drinking or the smoking. And it didn't really have anything to do with his cousin, although he knew Dennis would never have the same hold over him after that night. Not so much because William would see him differently, but because Dennis would think he did.

William rose and went to the back door and called. Freddie's tail thumped a few times on the porch and then William heard him rise and the click of his toenails as he came out of the shadows from the far corner. Freddie hesitated, then entered through the open door into the normally forbidden house. William lead him gently by the hair around his neck to his room, and half lifted, half pushed the confused dog onto the bed. Then he slid in between the sheets, pulled the dog in close so he could scratch at its belly, and listened to the soft thump thump of its tail on the blanket.

The Woman and the Maitre d'

PART ONE: WHAT WAS EXPECTED

The owner of the café smiled without heart at the waiter standing opposite him at the bar. "She's still a good woman, Emile," he told the waiter, "but she's no longer the woman I married."

Emile smiled sympathetically. He felt for the owner, but didn't know how to help him. Emile had a good wife with a job of her own who took good care of their three sons.

"Maybe you should have children."

The owner took a sip of his whiskey and laid the glass on the bar. His hands and his eyes remained with the glass. "I think she may be sleeping with another man."

Emile knew she was. He knew who she was sleeping with and where and how often. The other man was the maître d' at the restaurant of one of the large hotels in the city, and Emile had known him for many years. The maître d' was not a bad sort of man, but he often slept with the wives of other men.

"I don't think you have anything to worry about, monsieur. Your wife's a good woman who cares for you very much."

The owner shook his head. "It's very kind of you to say so, but I think you're mistaken, Emile." He finished his drink and grabbed the bottle and refilled his glass. When he tried to add to Emile's, the waiter placed his hand over the top, but the owner simply used the bottle to push his hand away. "Let me at least do this for you. Let me give you one good drunk while I complain."

Emile raised his glass to the owner. "You owe me nothing," he said, and drained the glass. The owner filled it again.

"You've heard nothing, then? Of my wife, I mean."

Emile shook his head. "No. Nothing."

"C'est bien," said the owner. "If you did, you'd tell me."

The following day the news of their disappearance surprised even Emile. He found the owner seated at a table in the corner of the café. A bottle of whiskey, not the one from the previous evening, sat on the table between his arms and the owner was very drunk. There were no patrons yet and Emile walked to the owner's table. "Are you all right, monsieur?"

The owner raised his head and looked at Emile. "She did what I've always known she would do," he said. "I don't know why I should be surprised. She simply did what I always knew she would do."

"Perhaps you should go home, monsieur. There's nothing for you to do here."

The owner raised his glass and smiled at it. "I can always drink here." He drained the glass and filled it again. His aim was still good and none was spilt. "I have nothing to go home for. I would only go down the hill to that bastard Andre's place. Besides," the owner said, pausing to light a cigarette, "here you can't ask me to leave - no matter how badly I behave."

Emile shrugged his shoulders. There was nothing for him to do. He'd seen the owner like this before and there was truly nothing he could do. "I'll get the café ready. Patrons will be arriving soon," he told the owner. "If you need anything, monsieur, call me," he said, and left the owner alone with his bottle and his thoughts and his cigarette burning in the ashtray.

PART TWO: AT THE TOP OF THE HILL

The old man trudged slowly up the hill toward the café, the heels of his pants dragging on the concrete behind him. His long, black overcoat hung heavily from his shoulders, the tattered edges brushing softly against his legs making a swishing sound that could not be heard above the noises of the night.

The owner of the café, who was leaning against a lamppost that bordered his establishment and smoking a cigarette, watched the old man's approach. The old man puffed his way up the hill and the owner puffed his cigarette and the end glowed against the night.

Behind the owner a group of Americans, who'd been in the café for several hours, drank and laughed and spoke in loud, forceful tones. They yelled for the waiter and the owner turned to watch Emile approach the table wearing his smile like a veil. These Americans were not good patrons, the owner thought. Although they were spending a large sum of money in his café, they'd been too loud for his regulars, who'd left with apologetic smiles and shrugs toward the owner and Emile and had gone down the hill to sit in Andre's. Andre's was almost as good and clean as his own café, but Andre would not be there to greet them or to exchange opinions on the affairs of their friends and the state of their country.

Nor would Andre sit with them when invited and share a whiskey and a cigarette and tell them of his wife who'd been unwilling to help in the café because she preferred to dress in expensive clothes and be seen at parties, or how she'd disappeared with the maître d' from Le Palais and was now living in the south where she would find someone rich to leave the maître d' for.

As the old man neared the café, one of the American women

spotted him and, immediately, all American eyes were turned toward him. Emile left to fetch another bottle of wine from the cellar.

The woman turned to her companions. "He's so cute." She spoke loudly enough for the owner, but not for the old man, to hear.

"He's just what I'd imagined them to look like," added another.

One of the American men cleared his throat but kept his eyes on the old man. "He's obviously a veteran. Probably of the First World War. Maybe the Second as well. You can see he has medals pinned to his coat." He then turned back to his companions and all eyes focused upon him. "That's something I'll never understand. How these damn Frenchmen can get medals when it was us who had to come over and save their butts. Not that we weren't happy to do it, mind you."

"Oh. Were you in the war?" one of the women asked him.

"Not exactly. I was more what you'd call stateside support services."

"Henry has flat feet," another woman explained.

Henry nodded in agreement. "Yes. A damn shame. Horrible cross to bear. I wouldn't wish it on anyone."

The old man looked at no one as he took a seat on the bench that had its back against the small fence separating the café from the sidewalk. The Americans could no longer see his face, only the turned-up collar of his overcoat and the beret that allowed a few wisps of grey to shine in the light from the lamps.

The old man sat on the bench and remembered two days before when he'd been in the stands watching the military planes fly overhead and machinery had rumbled proudly before him and the militia had marched by and saluted in his direction because the President was seated only yards away. He remembered people he'd never met shaking his hand and thanking him for his contribution to the continued freedom of their country. And he remembered smiling politely and wishing for a drink.

Emile returned and opened the fresh bottle of fine red but the Americans only poured it into their glasses and left it there. They had decided to try the café down the hill as this one was too quiet. They paid their bill and tipped Emile handsomely and nodded their thanks to the owner. As they left they passed the old man and the men ignored him but the women all smiled at him with sympathy as to a naughty child whom they would love to have forgiven had they been in a position to do so.

As soon as they were past the old man, the Americans spoke loudly again and the women laughed at all of the words the men spoke. The owner could still hear them as they reached the bottom of the hill and turned to enter Andre's.

The owner entered his own café and dealt with the money the Americans had left and then went out to help Emile clear away the mess that lay on the table. He spoke quietly to Emile as they worked, and glanced only periodically at the old man's back.

Emile said little and did not complain of the Americans for he knew that would only anger the owner who believed all customers were equal. Besides, both he and the café had made good money.

When the table was cleared the owner returned outside with a carafe of red and placed it on a table with a plate of meats and cheeses and a fresh baguette. He tapped on the old man's shoulder and motioned toward the table. "Pour toi, mon vieux," he said quietly. Not waiting for a reply, the owner turned and disappeared into his café, closing the door behind him.

The owner could hear Emile and the dishwasher talking quietly in the kitchen and he went behind the bar and poured himself a whiskey to take the edge from the night. He had a sip and turned and walked to the door where he flicked off all but one of the light switches. Taking a chair from a table, he turned it toward the window and sat to light a cigarette.

He let the smoke drift lazily from his mouth and looked out the window at the old man eating slowly at the table, his medals glimmering as he moved under the solitary lamp that still burned in the late evening dark.

PART THREE: AN AFTERTHOUGHT

The train ride was long and the man spoke to few and drank many. At Lyons he decided that finding his wife and her lover on a beach in Nice was not the right thing to do and he disembarked from the train. He could see no reason why he shouldn't still enjoy the Mediterranean sun and made a quick decision at the ticket window. He chose a small town on the Spanish coast and settled into his seat to wait with a fine selection of red wines.

Upon his arrival he was pleased to see posters for bull fights which were to take place that afternoon. Although he'd been to Spain many times, the fights had always eluded him. As there was very little time before the fights began, he took a room at the first hotel he found.

After pausing briefly to drop off his bag and to treat himself to a whiskey in the hotel bar, he walked toward the ring, stopping to buy cigarettes and to buy wine at a store that filled bottles from great caskets that lined the walls. Looking forward to the fights, he drank as he walked and felt happy to be in the late afternoon sun and for not being a fool and going to his wife.

At the ring he paid for a seat in the shade but sat in the sun which had felt good as he'd walked. He chose a seat beside two younger men, but after they refused his offer of wine the second time he moved forward to sit with three boys. One of the boys was the son of the man who opened the gate that led the bulls to their deaths.

The boys were fascinated by the foreigner sitting with them and explained the fights so he'd know the best parts. The last bull was particularly good and the crowd chanted "Toro! Toro!" and booed the matador.

Finally, after the matador had aimed his sword badly three times, the bull collapsed at the side of the ring and the matador closed in for his prize. He stood unsteadily beside the bull, its ear in one hand, while with the other he began to saw at the hair and flesh.

Suddenly, the bull reared its immense head, nearly striking the bad matador, and struggled to its feet. But the picadors moved in quickly and stuck the bull with their piques until his knees collapsed beneath his proud, black body and the matador once again sawed at its flesh while the blood poured from its nose and stained the ground before it.

When he was finished the matador raised the ear above his head and waved it at the crowd who made no noise while the picadors patted their horses and did not look, and the man felt badly and didn't watch for even he knew the bull had lost even though it had not been beaten.

That was the last fight and the man left the ring with the rest of the silent crowd and walked to the ocean where he stripped naked and had a long swim to try and shake the bad feeling that ran through his body.

When he got out of the water, he sat for a long time on the beach with no clothes and drank the remainder of his wine and thought not of his wife but of the bull and its bad luck to have been born so strong and good and of the matador who had been proud of what he had not done.

Later, the man was very drunk in a bar and found a whore who didn't care that his wife had left him or that a bull had been killed badly or that the man could not perform as a man, as long he paid her in American.

And the man didn't think of his wife or the bull or of the hotel manager who swore at him as he led the woman through the lobby.

the tiny kitchen

On weekends he saw a woman he'd met at an art gallery function. She had a steady job and a steady income and lived in a nice apartment filled with nice things. They went out for dinners and shows and walked hand in hand from shop to shop and made love whenever they felt like it and his journal lay closed in his back pack where he placed it on Fridays before the drive to the city.

During the week he spent his nights alone with a French vin de table or a litre of cheap Canadian and tried to write. When the words stopped coming he'd phone Katie and ask if she was not busy if he could come over. Katie always said yes, even if she was busy, because that's what people do when they're in love.

They drank scotch and he'd tell her about his weekend. She listened because she'd gotten her last boyfriend by being the other woman first and was hoping history would repeat itself. They drank her scotch at a table in her tiny kitchen and read their writing to each other until they were drunk and no longer making sense of Eagleton and the post-modern dilemma and then Katie would rise and straddle his lap and they'd hump fully clothed, just his fly open and Katie's skirt hoisted, panties pushed to the side. And it would be rough and never tender.

In the morning when she asked, he'd reply, "Of course. We'll always be friends. Just not that kind, that's all."

Then he'd leave and walk home with a hangover and write in his journal how bad he was feeling for the woman with the nice things and how bad he was feeling for himself for needing the woman with the table in the tiny kitchen.

Velvet Hides An Empty Breast

The evening Constance Newell dreaded finally arrived and she prepared for it with meticulous care.

She ran a brush through the remaining wisps of her grey, cotton-candy hair one last time. Studied her disappointing reflection in the mirror above the dressing table. Swivelled her head with bird-like jerkiness to appraise it from all angles. A single strand of pearls would be perfect above the clean, crew-neck of her rose Chanel suit. Not too showy. Didn't want to appear gauche. Yes. A single strand would add just the right touch. Would distract lingering eyes from the evidence of her age.

Her own eyes lingered for a moment on a silver-framed photograph that stood on the table. A group photo. Her children. At the time of the photo, still intact. Still four in number.

The fingers of her left hand brushed against the glass that stood between her and the picture. A boy and a girl, seven and nine respectively, are seated on a park bench, hands folded neatly in their laps. Another boy and girl, fourteen and eleven, stand behind them, crossed hands held the way the naked protect their sex. When ... why ... did they move them? Behind is a park, or at least a picture of a park. No one could pretend not to know the background was false.

Constance could hear Mr. Newell in the kitchen below. The refrigerator door. Rummaging for ice. The tell-tale tinkle of glasses.

She descended the stairwell slowly, carefully. Gripped the

banister for support. Sought the drink in Robert's hand.

He watched her sip. "How's that?"

Constance lifted her glass in a vague toast. "Fine. Just dandy. Yes. Thank you."

She turned toward the television. A half-familiar face, surrounded by starving children, flickered across the screen. Africa? Were they still starving in Biafra? Did Biafra still even exist?

"God, Robert. Can't you find something a little more pleasant?" She lit a cigarette.

"Are you sure you're up to this?"

"If I don't go now, I never will. I'm fine." But Constance felt far from fine. It had been a long time since she'd felt fine.

She turned away and waved her glass over her shoulder. "I'll certainly need another one of these before we go."

****

"Damn." Constance jammed her cigarette in the car's ashtray. She was what people refer to as an angry smoker. Inhaled deep and hard. Wrestled the smoke from each cigarette. Flicked the filters with her thumbnail in quick, decisive motions. Impaled spent butts upon their own red fire with an almost sadistic relish.

"What's wrong now?"

"Nothing. My glass just left a wet circle on my skirt, that's all." She dabbed at the mark with a tissue. "And what's that supposed to mean?"

"What's what supposed to mean?"

"Now. You said now. What's wrong now."

"It wasn't supposed to mean anything."

"It certainly didn't sound like it wasn't supposed to mean

anything." Constance lit another cigarette.

"Tonight might be nice," Robert ventured.

"Why do you say that?"

"No reason. It just might be, that's all. Be interesting to see the kids' place. They've been there almost two years."

"Well, I don't know why you think this will be any different than it's been with the others. They're all so... I don't know. And Peter's hair. Ghastly. Just ghastly. I won't even say what I think of his earring."

Constance was greatly troubled by her children's choices of partners. So much so that sometimes it was just too painful to not say anything.

"Oh, Peter's all right. Just different."

"And the wedding. You'd have thought his family paid for it." Constance took a sip of her drink, being careful to– cup the bottom with her hand that held the cigarette. "Where did Peter get off, picking the master of ceremonies? I can't believe Jennifer let him. That was supposed to be from our side."

"Well, we can't do anything about it now."

"No. But I've half a mind to tell them what I thought of that. God. And when I think of the time devoted to his family's speeches. What do you suppose our friends thought of that? I'm sure Millie Crawford had loads to say."

"Don't think about it, then. You'll only get upset."

"I don't want to think about it," Constance said. "Don't think for one minute I want to. But I just can't help it. After what we paid. It just makes me so angry."

"Perhaps it was a little one-sided."

"And he wore that damn earring. Could you believe it? After I asked him not to. His own wedding day and he wore that damn earring. I'll bet Millie had a field day with that."

"If you were so worried about what Millie Crawford was going to say, why in God's name did you invite her?"

"Why ... what a question. She's one of my oldest and dearest friends. Honestly, sometimes..."

****

The lane that led to the farmhouse was a quarter of a mile long. By the time the car stopped, the kids, along with Peter's parents, were assembled on the porch to greet them.

"God," Constance said. "What is that woman wearing?"

Her door swung open and Peter's father plucked Constance from her seat.

"So lovely to see you. Yes, yes. Just dandy. This is wonderful. Wonderful." Constance shook the hand Peter's mother, Peggy, extended toward her. Offered her cheek for Jennifer to kiss.

The farmhouse was an old, stone structure common to that area north of the city. One square block two storeys high, a large one-storey wing for the kitchen.

Recently renovated, the wing now housed a living room with a fireplace at one end, a kitchen at the other. They were separated by an island with a sink and a dining table.

Must be wonderful for dinner parties, Constance thought. Always pleasant to watch your food being prepared. Piles of dirty dishes hovering behind as you eat.

"Oh, yes, Dear. This open concept is so much nicer. Keeps everyone together. No. That's right. No sense being cooped up alone in the kitchen.

"Perhaps I could have the grand tour in a moment, after I've had a chance to sit and rest."

Constance turned to Peter. "Would you be a dear and pour a nice vodka and soda before you sit down? On second thought, maybe you'd better let Robert do it. He knows just the way I like them. Robert?"

At Jennifer's urging, Peter brought forward a painting for Constance to see.

"It's Jen," he explained. "As a child."

"Oh, isn't that marvellous. Yes, I see it now. The eyes aren't quite right. And the hairs a little off. But I see it now. Yes. That's Jennifer. Marvellous. Just Dandy. Robert. It's Jennifer."

"So it is." Robert said. "Well done." He handed Constance her drink.

Peter propped the painting against the wall, and clapped his hands together. "Anyone else? Dad? Dinner will be a few more minutes."

"Well," Peggy said. "This is lovely. It's so nice to see you. It's just rotten sometimes. The way you meet people at weddings and never see them again."

"Isn't it though," Constance said. "This is lovely."

"The wedding was beautiful, didn't you think?"

"Beautiful. Yes. Just dandy. The club always does a marvellous job."

"You've had weddings there before?"

"Not weddings. Geoff was married in a church. But the reception was at the club."

"I think a church wedding would have been nice. I've always believed in church weddings."

"Of course, if it wasn't what they wanted ... I suppose the club was fine."

"Oh, my. Yes. Your club did a marvellous job."

"Yes. Just dandy. But there's nothing like a wedding in a church. Makes it so much more official."

"Still, if it wasn't what they wanted... At least they're no longer living in sin."

"Robert ..." Constance waved her empty glass.

****

The dining table was antique pine with boards that ran crossways, each at its own level. The result was each dish balanced precariously as though floating atop frozen waves.

"A fine piece of meat, Peter," his father said.

"Certainly is," agreed Robert. "Nicely barbecued. Don't you think so, Constance?"

"Yes. I'm sure it is. Just dandy. Of course, I prefer it cooked a little more."

"I can put it back on the fire," Peter offered. "Only take a minute."

"Nonsense. This is fine. You just stay right where you are. This is just dandy. It's only a little underdone for my liking, that's all."

"Are you sure. Really. It'll only take a minute. It's no bother."

"No. I'm quite sure. This is just fine." Constance examined the piece on the end of her fork. "It's really only slightly underdone. I'm sure most people love it this way."

Peter rose. "Don't be silly. I'll cook it little more."

"Well ... if you're sure it's no bother."

"None at all."

When her meat was returned, Constance poked at it

tentatively.

"Is it better, Mother?"

"Oh, yes, Jennifer. Much so. Thank you. Yes, that's just dandy. I guess I'm just not that fond of beef."

When the others at the table began discussing golf courses, Peggy turned to Constance. "Are you still able to play?"

"No. Not at all. Not that I wouldn't love to. I would still love to."

"How are ... things?"

"Ghastly. I try to ignore it mostly, but that doesn't always work. Nor do the pills. I'm on the strongest they can give you, but they just don't seem to do much good anymore. Would you mind filling my wine? I'm afraid even that has become a chore."

"Well, it's lovely you could make it today. I know the kids were looking forward to having you see the farm."

"Wouldn't have missed it for the world. It really is very lovely. Just dandy. Although I'm not sure you could get me to live with all the dirt."

"No. That's true. It's not like the city. But, my goodness, the fresh air."

"I noticed a smell when we arrived. Does it often smell like that?"

Peggy laughed. "Only when it's time to spread the manure."

Constance winced. "Yes. Of course. That's what it would be, wouldn't it?"

Laughter came from the opposite end of the table.

****

Constance listened with little interest to the dinner conversation. Drank to ease the pain. The never ending pain in her body. Her body that had recently decided arthritis was not enough.

And now she was drunk. She motioned for Peggy to fill her wine glass, lit cigarette dangling dangerously from her lips. Her best impression of a young Lauren Bacall. It was only when it fell headlong into her glass that she became aware of the magnitude of the ash that had gripped tenaciously to her cigarette.

"Damn. This cigarette's gone and ruined a perfectly good glass of wine."

Jennifer rose quickly. "Don't worry about it. There's plenty. I'll get you a new glass. Can you reach the ashtray?"

"Of course I can reach the ashtray. It's not the damned ashtray. It's these damned cigarettes. They're not my usual brand, you know. These are not made very well."

Jenny looked at the pack. Recognized them as the brand she'd been smoking all her life. "Of course, Mother."

"Of course, Mother," Constance mimicked. "Of course. Oh, why are you all so cruel to me. It wasn't my damn fault."

No one had said it was.

It wasn't my fault!

****

Constance drew fiercely on her cigarette. "Well, you certainly seemed to be having fun at your end of the table."

"Peter's father seems a fine sort of fellow."

"Well, I can't imagine what you'd have in common with him if he's anything like his wife, which I believe he must be after that ghastly speech he gave at the wedding. God. What a common woman. She actually mentioned manure at the table."

She waited for a reply. Was irritated not to receive one.

"She brought up the fact that James still hasn't married even though they have children."

"Did she? What did she say?"

"She said that at least Peter and Jennifer were no longer living in sin."

"And ...?"

"And ... that's all. But I knew what she was thinking. She might as well have said it aloud and laughed in my face."

"I'm sure she meant nothing by it. She doesn't seem the type."

"Honestly, Robert. What did we do wrong? All of our children, every last one of them, have picked the most common people. John wouldn't have."

"John's dead. Who knows what he would have done."

"Well, it's no fault of mine. I did everything a mother's supposed to do."

"Yes. I'm sure you did."

"What's that supposed to mean: I'm sure you did. Are you saying you were any better? That it's my fault?"

"It wasn't anyone's fault. John just did what we always knew he would do. Christ, he tried it enough times."

"You're damn right it wasn't my fault. Maybe if you'd been around a little more instead of always at the office."

"Why are you doing this, Constance? Why do you always do this?"

"I'm sure I don't know what you're talking about."

"You always torture us about John." Robert took a deep breath. "John is gone. It's nobody's fault. No one could help him."

"Well, it certainly wasn't my fault."

"No one said it was."

"That damn therapist just about did."

"He said no such thing."

"If we hadn't stopped seeing him he would have. He was certainly working towards it. That's why I made us stop going. He was crazier than John."

"John wasn't crazy."

"He certainly acted it. Why else would he have done what he did? Why else, Robert? Why else would he done that to us?"

"I don't know, Constance. I really don't know. He was confused, that's all. He was just confused."

"And now the others are all married to horrid people and John's dead and my joints ache all the time and everything that used to make us happy is gone."

"No one is married to anyone horrid, Constance."

****

The following morning Constance felt much better. A tiny vodka and soda with her pills, and yes, things were much better. By the time Millie called, Constance was almost happy.

"Oh, Millie. It was a lovely evening. Just marvellous. I tell you, that Peggy Dodd is a wit. Why, she had me chuckling all night long.

"Oh, he is. Very handsome. That's where Peter gets his good looks.

"I know. Isn't his earring terribly avant garde. And that he wore it at the wedding and all. That younger generation. I dare say, they're much more adventurous than we ever were.

"I thought it was a very dashing touch, too. Yes. Just like Errol Flynn in that pirate film.

"Didn't he? I could have sworn he had an earring. Not even in the pirate film? Are you certain? Well, if he didn't, he should have. Everyone knows pirates wore earrings.

"Yes, that's what I said. Peter teaches at the university. Oh, you did. You're certain you heard him say high school? Oh, I'm sure you must be mistaken, Dear. I ought to know. I am his mother-in-law.

"Well, I'm sure he was talking about someone else or you misunderstood. You know how you have a tendency to only listen to half of what's being said.

"I'm sure I don't know what you mean. I am not being like that. I'm merely stating a fact, Millie.

"Now, Millie ... Millie! That's quite enough. That's no way for friends to speak to one another.

"Of course we are, Dear. Always have been. Always will be.

"Yes, thank you. The wedding was lovely, wasn't it? No church for those two.

"I know. I know. Isn't it a hoot? But what do kids these days want with formality?

"You knew the minister was Peter's uncle, didn't you, Dear?

"Yes, exactly. Quite religious, I believe. But not enough to be rude.

"Oh, but weren't they. Marvellous speeches. Just marvellous. Isn't his family a hoot?

"Yes, his father's a marvellous speaker. Quite eloquent, I thought. He's an engineer with one of the largest firms in town, you know.

"I can't recall the name. But Robert knows them and says they're among the best.

"The M.C.? Oh, he was good, wasn't he? Just dandy. He's a

good friend of both the children and we all thought who better for the job than him.

"One sided? Oh, Dear. You must be mistaken. I thought it was the perfect balance.

"Oh, I'm sure your mistaken. I didn't think he was rough at all. Perhaps you were the one who'd had a glass too many, Dear.

"I am not being that way again. I only said it because I happened to notice you hovering around the bar more often than not.

"There's no reason to get defensive, Dear. I merely made an observation. I'm sure I didn't mean anything of the sort by it. But you know as well as I do that you've had your moments in the past.

"For example? For example, at the Henrickson's Christmas party. The way you draped yourself over Don Sadler was a bit much, don't you think? You said as much yourself the next day. And his wife only just out of the hospital.

"Well, I did mention it to you, Dear.

"Millie! If you can't control yourself, I don't see how I'm supposed to.

"Now, now Millie. Don't start crying. Yes, Dear. I know it's not easy being on your own. Especially when you're always hearing the marvellous time Bill is having with his new wife. Why, just last week I heard they were in the Caribbean scuba div...

"Of course, Dear. You're absolutely right. That was very thoughtless of me.

"And now, you must tell me. How's Susan and her husband ... I'm so sorry, Millie. I've forgotten his name.

"That's right. Douglas. Yes. He's a mechanic, isn't he?

"Owns a dealership. Of course. You're absolutely right. Toyota, isn't it?

"Volvo? Of course it is. You're absolutely right. Honestly. I don't know where my memory has gone these days.

"Lunch? Of course, Dear. I'd love to.

"Oh, I'm terribly sorry. I'm afraid I can't on Tuesday. I'm having lunch with Bill's new wife."

The Unfailing Grey

Evan placed his feet carefully into the footprints before him. He listened to each scrunch of the snow under his boots and hoped his prey would not hear. Paused to shift his rifle, which was growing cold and heavy, from his left hand to his right.

Evan knew his prey could not be far ahead. Its tracks remained as yet uncovered by the snow that fell large and silent. Soon, Evan thought. Soon it'll be in my sights.

"Goddamn it, Evan. Would you hurry up."

Evan looked up to where his sister stood waiting with her usual look of adolescent disgust. Everything pretty well disgusted Adrienne these days. Even Evan.

"And stop dragging your skis."

As Evan caught up, Adrienne turned from him and together they trudged south along 12th Avenue as they did almost every shrunken Saturday of the long Milletteville winter. Crunched their way past the brick houses, early-morning colourless and silent, smoke from their chimneys drifting upward until it vanished amongst the snow that fell unhurried toward earth. Crunched their way past the Catholic churches that stood dark and ominous set back on their block-long lots.

Evan had been in one of the churches with Jean Marc, his next door neighbour. They'd gone for a youth activity organised by the priests. Evan felt small and insignificant enveloped by the church's immenseness. The walls stretched effortlessly far above him to a ceiling sweeping cold and distant. The boys' whispered voices illicit among the echo of those raised by the priests.

The priests were friendly enough, but Evan sensed their disapproval of him, their disapproval of all that occurred outside their own hallowed halls. Maybe he'd imagined it. Jean Marc continually told him horror stories of the disciplinary actions taken by the priests. Like the boy whose thumb had been broken when a priest swung down hard with a ruler for writing with his left hand. Evan was unsure whether he believed all his friend told him, but he was glad he was a Protestant all the same, and it would be a trip to Europe many years later before he would step foot in another Catholic church.

Evan had visited his own Protestant minister's home once, after church with his parents. The minister's wife greeted them at the door dressed like any mother. Evan was disappointed. He wasn't sure what he'd expected. Something different. Maybe a cloak like her husband's.

Before lunch the minister showed them artefacts he'd brought back from the Second World War. When he held up a grenade Evan had run from the room. He'd been very young then.

There weren't many Protestants in Milletteville. There weren't many English. Evan's own school ran from kindergarten through high school and had less than three hundred students.

Evan continued to walk in slow, exaggerated steps. Stretched his legs hard to drop his feet straight down into the footprints his sister left before him without touching the sides. They walked and did not talk. There was no wind and the bitter cold that bit at Evan's cheeks remained outside his bulky layers of clothing.

Ahead, at the corner of 123rd, a figure huddled. "There's your girlfriend," Adrienne said.

"Shut up." Evan wanted to say more, but he knew it was useless. Adrienne would only twist his words every which way and he'd get more and more frustrated. It was like that with Adrienne. She wasn't afraid to say anything.

A single ski stuck out of the snowbank behind the figure. The snow held the outline of the other ski and her ski poles where they'd fallen. In her hand hung a pair of ski boots clamped into a metal carrying rack.

The figure spoke. "Can you believe how cold it is? I can't believe our parents make us go out in this."

"Merde. Believe it," Adrienne said. "My father's still in bed and I bet my mother's back in with him. They're probably doing it right now."

Hilary giggled. "You're terrible. Isn't she terrible, Evan?"

Evan said nothing.

"Let's go." Adrienne said. "I'm freezing my ass off."

****

The girls walked ahead of Evan who hoisted his skis to his shoulder so they would no longer drag. He ignored the girls' talk. Ignored Hilary's attempts to include him in their conversation. Hilary was nothing like his sister. As far as Evan was concerned, Adrienne had everything. She got A's without studying and had a reputation as a bit of a rebel. Everyone wanted to be her friend. Hilary was smart too, but there was nothing remotely rebellious about her. Evan was pretty sure Adrienne only spoke to her because they were in the same class and because it was better than talking to him.

By the time they reached the end of 12th, past the last of the greyed houses, they were part of a small procession of alike-suited kids. They turned east onto the dirt lane that led into the small valley where their classes met. There was only one slope with a single rope tow driven by an old truck engine that sputtered and spat at the bottom of the hill.

The first day they'd been separated into groups by ability. Adrienne was in an intermediate class and skied from the top of the slope. Hilary was in the same class as Evan even though she was older. They got off half way where the slope remained gentle.

They stood their skis and poles in a rack and entered the small wooden hut that served as a lodge. Some faces turned to watch them pass, and there were a few nods of acknowledgement, but no one spoke to them. They chose an empty table and sat to replace their snow boots with ski boots. Evan watched Hilary struggle to reach her laces and pull them tight, her snowsuit straining at the seams, the material stretched flat and tight over her corpulent body. He looked away and thought of Kyle's laughter when he heard Hilary was in Evan's class.

"I didn't know pigs could ski," he said.

Evan watched beads of sweat appear on Hilary's brow. She looked up from her task and smiled at him. "It's so warm in here." She tried to blow the hair back from her brow, then used her hand to tuck it under her toque when it remained stuck to her perspiration sodden forehead.

Evan wanted to tell her it might help if she removed her hat, if she pulled off her jacket like he and Adrienne had done, but he sensed she wouldn't want to. That it would be more trouble than it was worth. He gave a brief half-smile in agreement. Adrienne looked up and rolled her eyes, then tugged on her laces one final time before tying a knot.

Outside, posts with cut-outs of animals were planted in the snow in a semi-circle. Hilary and Evan dropped their equipment at the picture of a seal balancing a ball on its nose and without a word Adrienne left them and walked toward the cut-out of a polar bear.

At first Evan had liked that Hilary was in his class. It meant he wasn't the only English kid. Not that he couldn't speak French. Until he started school, his friends were the kids in his neighbourhood - all French. Ever since Evan could remember he'd been pointing at things and saying their names in English, while Jean Marc would do the same in French.

"Pants," Evan would say, tugging on his jeans.

"Pantalon," Jean Marc would reply.

No. It wasn't that Evan couldn't speak French. It was just nice to have someone he knew, someone English, in his class.

As they waited for the rest of their class and their instructor, Evan looked at Hilary. He looked at the way her skis and poles had scattered apart when she dropped them. Evan arranged his own equipment so that he could simply step into his skis and slip his hands through the straps of his poles, and then looked at Hilary expectantly, but she made no move to do the same. Simply smiled and looked around as though it was her first time there. He stooped to pick up her poles and stuck them in the snow beside her. She smiled again and thanked him, and he noticed she was still out of breath from changing.

"I guess we're the first ones again," Hilary said. "I can't believe Claude isn't here." She pronounced their instructor's name 'Clod,' the way English people often did. The way hockey announcers in Ontario did. "There he is."

She pointed at Claude as he strode toward them, skis perched effortlessly across one shoulder. Evan looked the other way. He didn't want Claude to think that he was a part of a committee that anxiously awaited his arrival.

"Bonjour, Clod," Hilary said, as soon as he was within hearing distance.

"Salut, Hilary. Evan." Claude lifted his arms. "We have good snow today. Où est ta soeur?"

"Avec sa classe." Evan nodded toward Adrienne's group and tried not to watch as Claude walked over to speak with her.

As the other students arrived, Evan scrapped the bottom of

each ski boot across the metal toe piece of his bindings to remove any snow. He slipped the toe under the front piece's upper ridge, reached behind and pulled the cable up and over the back of his boot, then pushed down on the front clamp pulling the cable tight against his heel. Once in, he lifted and shook each ski to test its secureness.

"You're so fast." Hilary was looking up at him from where she kneeled, still pushing down on the first of her clamps. "I can never close these things." She stood and looked at him helplessly. With a sigh Evan slid parallel to Hilary. Pushed the clamp closed, instructed her to place her foot in the second binding, and closed it.

"Thanks," she said. "I'm such a klutz, I don't know what I'd do without you, Evan."

The first lesson Evan had stood beside Hilary throughout. It seemed to be what everyone wanted. Let the two English kids buddy up. Learning to ski was hard enough without having to worry about your vocabulary. And at first that was fine with Evan.

But he was beginning to feel differently. Was now embarrassed by his association with Hilary. She didn't seem to be catching on to the sport the way Evan was. The way the rest of the class was. And what was worse, she didn't seem to mind. Each time Hilary fell she simply swivelled to her stomach, brought her knees up to her chest facing downhill, and rolled back up onto her feet with a smile. Then shook her head and laughed as though she couldn't believe she was that bad, but wasn't it a hoot.

For some reason he couldn't explain, whenever Hilary fell Evan felt she took him down with her.

They got off the rope tow and Claude instructed them to extend their arms like wings and they took off in a line. Evan was last, behind Hilary, and could see her leaning the wrong way, her weight shifting to the wrong ski. To the inside ski. When she flopped over onto her side, she reminded Evan of a scene in a movie where a group of boys sneaked up on sleeping cows and pushed them over. He hadn't found the movie funny, and he saw no humour here.

Evan did not want to stop, but he knew he must. In the fresh deep snow, Hilary would need help standing. She would need to be brushed off. And if he didn't do it, the class would stand at the bottom waiting for her all day. As it was, they would be waiting for the two English kids, and while he knew they would not blame him, he felt guilty as though he was at fault.

He pushed both heels out and came to a halt below the snow-laden Hilary. She smiled up at him and laughed. "What a klutz," she said. "When am I ever going to learn?"

Evan's weak smile changed to a grimace as his attempt to hoist Hilary to her feet failed. He could feel the rolling eyes of his classmates at the bottom.

Les Anglais. Toujours, nous attendons les Anglais.

Ignoring Hilary's protests to wait one second while she gathered her strength, Evan placed one hand in her arm pit and with the other yanked hard on her arm. Using his own body as a lever, he pulled the limp body of Hilary up and over his hip and held her high until her skis flopped around to face the same direction as her, and then dumped the surprised Hilary hard onto her feet.

She waved her hand about. She wanted to say something but couldn't catch her breath. Evan turned and left before she could speak.

****

"Where's Adrienne?"

Evan had seen Adrienne and Claude kissing around the corner of the chalet. "Staying to ski," he said.

Hilary looked away. "That was harder than last week," she said. "This new snow is making things miserable."

Evan wanted to say that snow was what skiing was all about. "You did really well."

She smiled. "Do you think so? I want so much to stay on my feet, but it scares me sometimes." At her corner she asked him in for hot chocolate.

The house was dark and quiet. Her parents were curling, Hilary explained. They took their hot chocolate into the den. "I know Adrienne was kissing Claude," Hilary said.

"Yeah, so."

"So nothing. I just didn't want you to think it bothered me." They sat awkward and silent for a moment. "Do you want to see something?"

"Sure."

Hilary led Evan down to the basement to her father's office. "He doesn't know I found these," she said, pulling two magazines from his desk drawer.

She opened them on the carpet where they sat and began to look at the pictures. The women were naked. Evan could see their breasts dangling. Could see tufts of hair just visible between their legs. "These women are beautiful," Hilary said, as much to herself as to Evan. "They could have any man in the world they want." They flipped through more pages. "Have you ever kissed a girl before?"

Evan was not about to tell her about being pinned down on the ground beneath his cousin and not being allowed up until they kissed. "No."

"Would you like to?"

"Yeah, I guess so," Evan replied, unsure of what she meant.

Hilary leaned forward and pressed her lips against his. Evan did not respond, but neither did he move away. He could feel his heart beating faster with a feeling not unlike panic.

Hilary pulled away and smiled and then kissed him again. This time, he felt her tongue worming its way between his lips, pushing at his teeth.

"Open your mouth," she said. "We're supposed to touch tongues."

He did as instructed and felt her tongue prodding and exploring his mouth. Felt it twirl around his own and then she was sucking his into her mouth. They fell back onto the floor, locked in their awkward and unfamiliar embrace.

And then Hilary took Evan's hand in hers and placed it on her breast. Evan gripped at it tentatively. He could feel the hard material of her bra beneath her turtleneck shirt and beneath that the soft malleable mound of her breast.

Hilary's mouth found his neck and he heard her breathing deep and heavy. He looked at the way his fingers pushed into her sweater, into her breast. Through the layers he found her nipple and tweaked it between his thumb and forefinger. Hilary gasped and he did it again.

His initial fear gone, Evan reached beneath her shirt and ran his fingers across her smooth skin. He moved his hand upward, toward her bra, but she stopped him. "Let me," she said. She sat up and lifted her sweater over her head and her large heavy breasts hung before him strapped in a white bra. She locked her eyes onto his, reached behind and unfastened her bra. Evan gasped as her breasts tumbled forward.

He reached out and cupped one in his hand. Hilary's eyes closed and she took a deep breath as he moved his hand around in a circular motion. He watched as her nipples grew with the attention. He looked at her face. Her eyes were again closed and he was surprised to see her lips parted in a tiny smile. Embarrassed, he pulled his hand away.

"Why did you stop?"

"I thought you were laughing at me."

"Don't be stupid," she said. Then she became very serious. "I'll take my pants off if you'll take off yours." Evan nodded dumbly.

He followed her example and stood and undid his pants. "We've got to do it at the same time," she said. "Underwear too."

They lowered their pants and Evan watched as a dark patch appeared between Hilary's legs. He looked down at his own small patch of hair and at his penis which swung semi-erect in the air before him. Moved his hands to cover it.

"Don't" she said. "I want to see it." He tensed as her hand closed over him. She seemed pleased as he grew in response to her touch. She guided his own hand between her legs. "See," she said. "There's nothing to be afraid of."

They knelt facing each other and she stroked Evan as he rubbed his hand across her groin. He felt the coarseness of her hair, and was amazed by the moist warmth.

Then Hilary let go of Evan and used both her hands to rub his hard against her mound. She leaned back so her breasts hung heavy to the sides. Her eyes were closed and her breathing was deep and heavy and the way her eyelids fluttered reminded Evan of a classmate who had small seizures, sometimes in the middle of class. Then she stopped his hand and her breasts heaved in short hungry gasps.

Hilary relaxed her grip and Evan pulled his hand out slowly, unsure of what he supposed to do, how he was supposed to feel. Hilary leaned forward and kissed him while her hand returned to his erection. He felt the pressure mounting inside him and then her mouth broke from his and they both watched his fluid gush forth and land on his chest and on her arm and Evan let out the breath he'd been holding as he raised his hips off the carpet to meet her hand.

After a moment, Hilary stood and got tissues from a box on her father's desk. She handed one to Evan and used another to dry her arm.

Evan cleaned himself. "I've got to go," he said.

"If you want." They replaced their clothes in silence and then Hilary put the magazines back in the drawer where she'd found them and walked Evan to the door. She sat on the stairs leading to the second floor and watched him dress. "I've never done that before," she said.

"I know." Evan tried to hurry without looking like he was. Pulled his boots onto the wrong feet, hoped Hilary hadn't noticed, and with a mumble slipped out the door.

****

That week Evan avoided Hilary at school. He passed her in the halls and pretended not to notice. Pretended to be looking elsewhere. He wasn't sure if he was imagining it or not, but he thought she was watching him.

On Thursday she approached him at his locker. He knelt and dug down in the bottom pretending he was looking for a book.

"You don't have to be scared of me," she said. "I haven't told anyone."

"I'm not scared."

"I know I'm not like your sister. Not beautiful like her. Not popular. But I thought we were friends."

"We are."

"Then why are you avoiding me? Every time I'm near, you look the other way."

He shrugged.

"I don't want anything from you," she said.

"I don't like you," Evan said. "I don't even like skiing with you."

He spoke into the locker. Did not know why he was saying these things. They weren't true. He looked up to take it back, but she was gone.

At recess, Evan told Kyle about it. But he said they'd only kissed. Kyle laughed. "Evan likes Piggy," he shouted, putting on a show for their pals. Normally, kids didn't make fun of older kids, but with Hilary it was different. She was fair game for all. She was too nice. Everyone knew it was safe. They knew there would never be any repercussions.

Evan walked away without a word. The more he defended himself, the worse it would get. Trust Kyle to be such an ignoramus. Tell him one thing and suddenly it's all over the school. He wasn't supposed to say anything to anyone. He was supposed to be Evan's best friend.

Evan entered the woods at the far side of the field behind the school. Sat beneath a tree. Saw his sister's gang gathered by the fence passing cigarettes among themselves. Adrienne looked at him with a puzzled expression on her face, but he turned away before she could signal to him. He was glad when she did not approach.

That night Adrienne entered Evan's room, something she now rarely did.

"What's up with you?" she asked.

"Nothing. Just doing my homework."

"Why were you moping in the woods?"

"No reason."

She walked around the room behind him and looked at the posters of sports figures on his wall. "These guys still your heroes?"

Evan shrugged. Watched her curiously, uncertain whether her presence was a good thing or bad.

"Guys can be the biggest jerks on the planet," Adrienne said, still looking at his posters. "especially if you have something they don't." She started to leave but paused at the door. "You should be flattered when someone with a brain takes an interest in a little dweeb like you."

The following Saturday Hilary was not standing on her corner when they arrived. Adrienne said nothing but kept walking as though Hilary was not supposed to be there.

"Shouldn't we wait?" Evan said.

"No."

With relief Evan saw Hilary standing by the seal ready for their lesson. When he came out she stood and looked off into the distance waiting for the class to start and did not return his greeting. During the lesson she stayed far away from him. Once he stopped to help her get up. "I can do it myself," she said. Struggled to her feet and pushed away without so much as a glance in his direction.

Afterward, she left quickly and he had to rush to catch her before she reached her corner.

"I'm sorry," he said as he ran up behind her. "I don't know why I said those things."

Hilary stopped. They were standing before a church and she seemed to be studying it. Then she turned toward him. He thought she might cry, or at least look sad, but her face was blank of all emotion. "I thought you were different," she said. "I thought you'd be nice. Like your sister. But you're nothing like her."

Then she turned and left him standing before the church that leaned toward him grey and unforgiving.

they stood in the parking lot

They stood in the parking lot, her arms clinging about his neck. "You're just going back because you don't want to live with me anymore."

He moved her face away from his and smiled. "I'm going back because I want us to have a good life," he said. But when he climbed in the car he recognized the sense of relief and knew she was right.

She called three weeks later, but by then he'd already heard rumours about her Florida trip and didn't feel so bad about treating her shabbily on the phone.

"I guess I caught you at a bad time," she said finally.

"No," he said too quickly. Then, "Yes. I guess I am kind of bogged down with homework. I'll call you later."

When he did call three months had passed and the hunger had left her voice. And then the week before he was to return she told him she was living with his old roommate.

He tried to sound disappointed at the news because he figured he was supposed to be. Then he thought about getting angry, but his heart just wasn't in it. So he pushed down on the button of the telephone very slowly until the line went dead.

The Diner

The bus jolted across the dirt shoulder and skidded to a halt on the blacktop outside the diner where it sat expectantly while the dust caught up in the wheel wells drifted by and settled. The driver pushed hard on the big steel knob and the door swung open. Eddie stood in the aisle bent low looking out the window at the diner while he waited for the others seated forward to lumber off with the awkwardness born of a long bout of sitting. Then he followed, stepping down and out of the protection of air-conditioning and tinted glass and stood squinting in the hot dry sun.

We stay here for one hour, the bus driver was telling them all. Get yourself something to eat and do whatever else it is you gotta do. There isn't another stop for over three hours. And don't go wandering off. We've got a schedule to keep and we can't be looking over hell's half acre for nobody.

Eddie stood by the bus and looked down the street into town. It looked like any other lakeside town he'd ever been to, the main street stretching itself a few blocks to accommodate shops brimming with antiques and handicrafts, racks of T-shirts out front on the sidewalk waving in the light breeze off the lake. Even the Value Mart had T-shirts and large wire mesh baskets of beach balls and multi-coloured blow up toys in various shapes and sizes. Eddie stood by the bus and squinted down the street until the driver called to him from the diner, reminding him they only had one hour. Eddie waved to show he was coming.

Inside Eddie chose a stool at the counter, swinging his leg over it in what he hoped looked like a comfortable gesture and settled on his haunches letting his back curve out and the weight of his body fall partially on his elbows which now rested on the counter.

What d'ya got? he asked the waitress when she approached. He smiled at her in a way he thought was teasing, but she just pointed with her pencil at the menu that stood wedged between the salt and pepper shakers and the bottle of sugar and said, take a look and let me know. She was a blonde with big hair and a tag that said Cheryl. She wasn't bad looking and reminded Eddie of the waitresses he'd seen in movies that the heroes always joked around with and he had the strangest urge to do the same. It was something Eddie did, trying to fit into places he didn't belong, imitating parts he'd seen in movies or read in books. He liked to think he belonged wherever he found himself.

So what's Norm's speciality? Eddie used the name Cheryl had called through the kitchen window. Cheryl eyed him for a brief second before yelling over her shoulder. Bus fellow here wants to know what your speciality is, Norm.

You're my speciality, Honey, a booming voice replied. You wish, Cheryl said not loud enough for Norm to hear. He makes a fine shepherd's pie, but that's all gone now. If I was you, I'd stick to the burgers and fries. Even Norm can't mess that up.

I heard that, the voice inside the window said.

Well then how come you can't hear nothing I ever order, Cheryl replied. She smiled and winked at Eddie as though he were a little boy even though in all likelihood Eddie was five years older than her.

Eddie watched Cheryl work as he waited for his burger and listened to her and Norm throw innocent barbs at one another without either of them taking the other seriously or worrying about who heard or what anyone thought about it. He watched her work and thought about how it must be nice to have a job where no one cares if you're having a bad day because they'd just make fun of it anyway and sooner or later you'd have to laugh and then you wouldn't be in a bad mood anymore. He watched the way Cheryl moved with a tired comfort through the diner and thought about how fine it would be to meet her outside at the end of her shift and to walk her home and to hear about the people that came into the restaurant that day and how every once in a while someone interesting or famous or maybe even both would come in and you'd have a good story to tell about how they wanted to take you to Hollywood and make you a star but you said no because you had everything you needed right here and a little fame would only ruin it all anyway.

When the burger was ready, Norm himself peered out the window and asked if Eddie was the fellow that wanted the burger and told Eddie how he was one lucky fellow because Cheryl wasn't lying when she said he made the best burger this side of Toronto. Then he laughed because he knew Cheryl had said no such thing and he knew Eddie knew so it was like they were sharing a little joke on Cheryl and Eddie felt so good he wanted to order a scotch or a beer but couldn't because the joint wasn't licensed and so he pulled the flask out of his jacket pocket and poured a little into his coffee when no one was looking.

When Cheryl had finished serving the others she came and leaned on the counter and asked where Eddie was from and he named a small town outside of Toronto even though he wasn't from there because he knew how people felt about people from the city and the reputation they had for being snobs.

Never heard of it, she said. Figured Eddie was from the city but then she should have known better because people from the city generally don't come in here, especially not on buses. People in the city all have their own cars, especially those jeeps, she said. Now you tell me what a person living in Toronto needs with a jeep? But Eddie just shook his head and said he didn't know either but it was a damn shame the way they polluted and everything, and Cheryl nodded her head in agreement and Eddie was feeling good that they were talking and agreeing on something, so he said, let's ask Norm but Norm didn't know either, but - and he came to the window to look at Eddie as he said this – he knew one thing. It was a bloody waste of good gas and good traction that the good people of Kowanie could use, not that they could afford it.

They all shook their heads in agreement and Eddie felt so good that he pulled his flask out again and tilted it towards Norm who smiled and said, don't mind if I do. Cheryl handed it to Norm and then back to Eddie refusing to take any herself, but pouring Eddie another half cup of coffee to go with his scotch and they each sort of smiled off into the distance and reflected upon the stupidity of Toronto people and their need for big jeeps and Eddie thought about how he'd like to walk Cheryl home and climb in between her big white thighs and stay there for a month of Sundays.

It was not like they'd miss him at the office. Hell, he was on precarious ground as it was. Sales was getting too damn technical, that was the problem. Everyone had a goddamned university degree for Christ's sake. What the hell that had to do with sales, Eddie would never know. What he did know was that kids ten years his junior were getting the jobs he'd always thought were meant for him and his paycheque wasn't getting any bigger even though his bills were. What would happen, he wondered, if he just didn't go home? The office would be rid of him, which they were probably trying to do anyway, and his wife could sleep with whomever she damn well pleased and he wouldn't have to hear about it the next week when an indiscreet but fully intended comment dropped from one of his friend's mouths. And his son, well Christ, his son barely spoke to him as it was. Probably take him a month to figure out Eddie was gone. Always moping about the house, grumbling about one thing or another. Sometimes Eddie would turn and catch his son peering at him with what Eddie could only describe as a sneer of revulsion. Eddie had even dreamed he woke up one night with a knife in his chest and his son standing over him smiling. It wasn't that Eddie didn't love the kid. He was Eddie's own flesh and blood, for God's sake. But sometimes he just didn't like him.

No, if Eddie disappeared on the road one day, he didn't think it would make much of a dent in anyone's life. And that, Eddie suddenly realised, was damned depressing. To think he'd slaved his whole life to get where he was, and where he was was butt-fuck nowhere. Forty-three years and he didn't even have a mother – god rest her soul – to miss him.

The voice of Cheryl asking what he did for a living brought Eddie back to his surroundings. He didn't want to tell her the truth, didn't want her to guess everything about him in one blink of an eye. A carpenter, he said, and it wasn't so far from the truth. Hadn't he built a new deck on their house just last summer. The boy was supposed to help him but, of course, never stuck around the house long enough to lift a single board and so Eddie been forced to hire the same fellow who'd done his neighbour Jack's deck a few weeks earlier. Eddie had stayed by his side the whole way, helping as he could and trying to emulate the easy way the carpenter had moved about the wood and moved about with his tools as though they were natural extensions of his arms. He'd even bought himself a good leather tool and nail pouch and had spent several evenings working the leather and scraping it against the red brick of his house until the leather looked old and worn and well used.

I build decks, he continued. Tool sheds. Small things like that.

Cheryl peered down at his hands. You got awfully smooth skin.

Business hasn't exactly been good, Eddie said, and Cheryl nodded her head and said ain't that always the truth and Eddie liked her even more for understanding the plight of the average working man and wanted to tell her that but knew there was no way to make her understand what he was thinking. Knew there was no way for her to know he wanted to be a carpenter for real and to live in a small town like Kowanie with a woman like her who understood that life wasn't always about having cars and televisions and fancy clothes to go to work in and giving dinner parties where people you don't give two shits about stand around your house drinking your booze while they judge your success by your possessions.

Eddie wanted to be a carpenter in this small town with her, with Cheryl. And if there was no other work then he'd get a job as a bag boy at the Value Mart down the street and that would be just fine because at the end of his shift he could walk one block and take his usual stool at the counter and everyone would say, Hi Eddie. How are you doing? and he'd tell them just fine and ask how they were and they'd talk about the weather and the Blue Jays or the Maple Leaf game the night before and discuss their chances of making the playoffs and he'd have a piece of lemon meringue pie while he waited for Cheryl and then they'd walk back to their place somewhere down by the lake and sit outside on their dock in each other's arms and watch the sun go down over Lake Superior and then go into the house and crawl into bed and make love the way only people really in love can, with her taking as much pleasure out of it as Eddie, instead of letting him do it the way a woman lets a man have a few beers and watch the ball game - because it's the easiest thing to do.

And Eddie looks up and wants to tell Cheryl these things because - who knows? – she might understand and say, you know, I've always been looking for those same things and then she'd tell Norm, I need the rest of the day off to discover my destiny and they'd walk off together right then and there and go back to her place and she'd make him a coffee or maybe they'd have a cold beer on the porch but they wouldn't even finish them before they'd tumble into her bed and make love like they knew they were supposed to be there together and then afterward they'd lie in bed for hours talking and then maybe later, after they made love again, this time slow and easy, they'd go back out onto the porch and sip a beer and watch the stars overhead and not say too much because there was no need to – but Eddie can't say a thing.

Suddenly the driver is at Eddie's elbow telling him to finish up his lunch because they have to leave in five minutes and Eddie yells goodbye to Norm through the kitchen window and Norm peeks through and gives him a wave and Cheryl at the cash smiles and tells him to take care and says be seeing you around and when he walks outside and sees all the fat asses waddling their way back toward the bus Eddie is damned if he's going to follow. Without a word he turns right and walks into town ignoring the driver's calls and steps through a corner doorway under a dead neon sign of a martini glass with cocktails scrawled across it and pauses on the threshold of the dark sanctuary.

After his eyes get used to the dark, Eddie walks to the bar and swings his leg lazily over a stool in his best western style approach and calls to the bartend for a scotch without too much ice because he doesn't want the thing going watery on him and then swings around to view his surroundings. He nods with satisfaction at the place he's chosen. This was more like it. Fuck the bus. Fuck the job. And most of all, fuck the family. What the hell did they know about him anyway?

This is a fine establishment you have here, friend, he told the barkeep as he swept up his glass from the bar. Eddie raised his drink in a toast. To it and your long and happy life, he said and then threw back his drink. The nectar of the god's, he said when he had caught his breath. Another please. Then Eddie turned to an old bugger seated two stools away. There was no time like the present to start making friends in what he had just decided was to be his new home. And you, my friend. What'll it be?

The old man eyed him suspiciously, then turned to the barkeep. Same as always, Brett. And don't give me that goddamned water-downed crap you try to pass off as whiskey, you cheap bastard.

Ain't nothing watered down in here except your brain, you stupid old fart.

Smartass cocksucker.

Shut up, you malignant tumour.

Eddie listened and smiled and reached for his glass as he felt the warmth of the whiskey spread through his chest.

Of Mutilated Wings

Marge is fading. When she looks in the mirror she can see through her body to the room beyond, can tell where every object is, can see every mark on the wall behind her. It makes perfect sense, accounts for Doug's behaviour.

****

Marge and Doug live in a small town typical of many small towns relying on one industry: it's dying. Everyone Marge knows is gone, moved away. No one wants to witness the death of their town if they can do otherwise. No one except Doug.

Doug's used to suffering. Long ago, he suffered through the misfortune of almost playing in the National Hockey League. He even practised with the Montreal Canadians - once - but the Second World War arrived and ruined his big chance.

Doug and Marge met while Doug was in boot camp. When camp ended, when the men he trained with sailed overseas, Doug remained behind. He was the best goalie their hockey team had ever seen, far too good to risk losing in Europe. This gave Doug and Marge a chance to fall in love. They married while the war was still ruining Doug's big chance.

Doug and Marge had a son soon after the war in Europe. Doug spent many hours coaching his son's hockey teams as he made his way through the minors. Finally, like his father, Doug Jr. almost played in the NHL. But Doug Jr. hated hockey.

At eighteen, he packed his bags and left home without a word.

****

Before Marge and Doug's town began its slow death, a social life existed. It centred mostly around the curling club, to which they belonged as non-playing members. There was also a golf course, but Doug could never see the point of chasing a small, white ball across the countryside. He liked the other name he'd heard for golf: whap-fuck. Both clubs closed as people escaped town, although rumours continue of the golf course reopening.

****

Marge used to play golf. When she was a teenager in Montreal her parents would take her to play on hot, summer days. But more than the golf she liked to hang out near the workshop while her parents relaxed in the bar. She liked to hang out by the workshop and watch the young men repairing equipment, taking breaks for quick smokes. She'd watch them deftly roll cigarettes with one hand, lighting them with matches cupped in the palms of their hands. And she'd watch them watching her. When her parents finally called to her from the front door of the clubhouse she'd turn from the boys and walk away, careful not to look back.

More forward than the others, one of the workers would wave and shout to Marge, and then smile at her discomfort, at her attempts to appear disinterested. His name was Stephan and Marge recognised his position of rank above the others by the way they listened and laughed when he spoke.

On one occasion, Marge disappointedly found no boys outside the workshop, but before she could turn away, Stephan emerged from within and motioned for her to enter. Marge followed into the darkness of the shop where Stephan now leaned against a bench smoking. He extended the cigarette towards her. The smoke assaulted her lungs, caused her chest to rack with spasms as she coughed. Stephan retrieved the cigarette from her hand, watching her with faint amusement.

Then he dropped the cigarette to the floor, squashed it under the toe of his boot and moved close to Marge. He grasped the back of her neck and leaned forward, pushed his mouth against hers. Marge could smell his sweat, could taste the smoke hot on his breath. As his tongue wormed its way between her teeth, Stephan's free hand searched for her breast through her light, cotton shirt, through the light, cotton bra she'd only begun to wear. Marge felt the blood rush to her face and a warm flush between her thighs. Her arms dangled, impotent at her sides, while Stephan's hand kneaded her breast and his tongue explored her open, unmoving mouth.

When voices signalled the arrival of other boys, Stephan's mouth broke from Marge's. She pushed him away roughly and rushed for the light of the doorway, shooting out past the startled intruders, and ran towards the clubhouse.

****

It's one o'clock in the afternoon and Doug has just risen. Marge thinks of Stephan as she watches Doug light his first cigarette of the day, the one he has with his first coffee. Marge watches Doug and thinks of Stephan and the summer they spent time together. She thinks of his long, tanned body and of the way he laughed at her amazement the first time he showed her his prick. She remembers how large it looked and how tiny her hand in comparison, stroking up and down the way Stephan showed her. She also thinks of the strength she felt when she realised the power her tiny hand held over Stephan.

Doug squashes his cigarette in the ashtray as Marge slips two fried eggs onto his plate. He unfolds the newspaper and flips to the sports section, checks to see if the experts agree with his analysis of last night's game. As he reads he slices the eggs open with his fork, then stabs at the broken yolk with his toast.

"I think I'll head to the mall," he says, without raising his head. He speaks as though Marge doesn't already know this, as though it's not what he does every day.

"Maybe I'll give Rejean a call. See if he wants to come."

Rejean lives in a retirement home only three blocks away and is Doug's only consistent companion. Together, they spend their afternoons sitting in the mall, smoking cigarettes and talking of days gone by. Like all good Québecois of his generation, Rejean is a Habs fan. He knows all of the players in Doug's stories, although most of these men are now dead.

After Doug leaves, Marge takes her memories and runs a bath. She adds oil to the water to help replace the moisture lost by her ageing skin. Removes her clothing and examines her reflection in the mirror above the sink. Ignoring the faint reflection of objects behind her, she concentrates on the way her skin sags beneath her chin. She's beginning to look like a grandmother, like her grandmother.

She turns away from the mirror, back to the water, back to her memories. Lies down in the tub and the water envelopes her body like a warm shroud. Her hands glide over the artificial smoothness of her skin, raising memories of the texture of Stephan's erect penis. Closing her eyes, Marge remembers the smoothness as it slid through her tiny fist, as it insisted its way between her sixteen-year-old thighs, and as it pushed at the entrance to her sex until her virginity gave way. And she remembers the warm flood erupting on her stomach as she lay shuddering beneath Stephan's heaving body.

Marge has slid forward and the faucet pounds water onto her forgotten sex. Her hands have found their way beneath the water, between her legs, and she rubs, frantically, searching for something she fears may be lost. Then her back arches as she reaches for the water and her body shudders with a rediscovered momentum.

****

When Doug returns from the mall, Marge is reading a book her friend, Connie, has given her. Younger than Marge, Connie is actually the daughter of one of Marge's uprooted friends. Connie didn't follow because she's married to a local businessman who's suffering through the death of his town. The novel concerns the trial of a woman who set her husband on fire while he lay asleep in bed. The woman's defence was the abuse her husband had inflicted upon her during their marriage.

As she reads, Marge finds herself wishing Doug would abuse her in some way, just a little.

Doug turns on the TV.

****

"There's talk of the Habs trading ..." and Doug names a player unknown to Marge. Aimed at the TV, his voice surprises her.

She doesn't know if the news is good or bad, so she waits for the commentary that will follow after Doug allows her to feel the gravity of the situation.

"They're damn fools," Doug finally continues. "They wouldn't know a good player if he bit them on the ass. I saw the same thing happen in '49 with ..." he names another unfamiliar player and rattles off a list of repercussions resulting from the ancient trade. Marge tries to return to her book but the television and Doug prove too great a distraction.

"Time to make dinner," she says, rising and dropping her book onto the end table.

****

Light from the television steals down the length of the hall and through the open door to Marge's bedroom. The clock reads 2:37 am. Doug is watching an old black and white film, not a classic though, just old. Doug does this every night. His life drifts from 1 pm to 4 am, intersecting with Marge's at only meal times.

Marge watches the light and listens to the faint voices coming from the television. She doesn't worry about the fading at night, for although transparent, her body remains solid. She tests this fact and her exploring hands stir the memory of her afternoon bath. She rolls to her side, her hands clamped snugly between her thighs, and watches the flickering light lick at the walls like flames.

****

Two days have passed since Doug tried to sit on Marge. She was seated in his chair. He didn't notice as he entered the room to watch the TV.

Marge had sat in his chair on purpose.

She's convinced the fading is worse than she'd originally thought.

****

Marge is wearing new clothes. A canary yellow shirt above a skirt of bright red with large, purple polka dots. Items she found in the bargain bins at Woolworth's.

"Christ," Doug says. "What the hell is that?"

"What's what?"

"That." His hand sweeps the length of Marge's figure. "What you're wearing."

"Nothing," she says. "Just something a little different. That's all."

Doug takes one last look before turning on the TV.

****

Marge sits before the bathroom mirror. Spread on the counter is a complete makeup kit she purchased this morning, while Doug slept. Slowly and methodically, Marge begins to apply the makeup to her translucent skin until the light no longer shines through her face, blocked by layers of mismatched colour.

When finished, Marge looks for holes, for spots where she can still make out the room beyond. Satisfied, she rises and dresses in the previous day's outfit, adding bright pink sneakers. She examines her legs. They don't seem faded, but she doesn't trust them. She pulls white stockings from her dresser, to be on the safe side.

****

Doug says she's going crazy. Better that, Marge thinks, than to disappear.

****

Doug Jr. disappeared. At eighteen, he packed his bags and left home. No note. No message. Not even a phone call to let them know he was all right.

For many weeks, Marge continued to set a place at the table for him, until Doug exploded with anger and she was forced to stop.

Marge still cooks for an extra mouth, but without Doug's knowledge.

****

Marge enters the coffee shop on la rue Principal, where her new friends call her "'ti-Marge." She likes the name, draws comfort from it. Somehow it confirms her existence, that she can be small and visible at the same time.

Marge has been coming here since the playoffs began. Doug stays home watching all the games on TSN, even those taped previously. At the coffee shop she drinks coffee and smokes cigarettes with her new friends, but mostly they talk about where they'd rather be.

****

Marge tells her new friends about Doug Jr. Sometimes she tells them he works long hours running a small hotel in Montreal. When he does visit, she says, he sleeps in the same bed he grew up in surrounded by pictures of himself playing hockey. There's also a large photo of his father posing in the classic goalie stance. Although he doesn't visit often, she says, Doug Jr. frequently phones, like a good son should.

Other times, Marge tells them he's dead.

She no longer knows which story to believe, no longer knows the truth.

****

Marge's coffee companions are Pierre and Chantal. On her second visit to the shop, Pierre took a seat across from Marge, held up a small, brown paper bag and smiled. Then he tilted the bag and Marge watched gold liquid tumble out of the bag and into her cup. She took a sip, returned the smile and thanked her new friend.

Today, Marge has the brown paper bag. Inside is a jar filled with rye from the liquor cabinet at home. Doug never drinks rye, so Marge is sure he won't notice.

She passes the bag to her two grateful companions, and then they talk of leaving. This has been the topic of conversation for several days, since the warm weather arrived. Nothing holds Pierre and Chantal here. They have no family and, several weeks behind in their rent, their landlord is threatening to evict them.

They're trying to convince Marge to accompany them to Montreal where money can still be made, either by work or by panhandling. And they know all the best spots for their kind. Shelters where they can get food, clothing, a bed. Perhaps Marge will even see her son.

****

Sometimes Marge and Doug discuss leaving their small town. Or rather, Marge talks and Doug ignores her. Comfortable with his routine, he sees no reason for change.

Doug thinks Marge's desire to leave is a phase, like the clothing. He offers her an aspirin and suggests she go to bed early, that she try to get more rest. He's certain things will look different in the morning.

Marge accepts the aspirin, but only because she has a headache. Too much rye, too many cigarettes. Dinner was almost late. Had the hockey game ended early, Doug might have noticed her absence.

****

Marge is cooking. She's been cooking for two days, ever since she cleaned the freezer. As she cooks, she places the results in individual packages, instant meals for one, ready for the microwave.

Marge has also been cleaning. While she waits for things to cook or bake, she pushes the vacuum, or scrubs the toilets, or washes the walls. She's even discarded her Canadian Living magazines, the ones with the recipes she intended to one day try.

Doug notices her flurry of activity, but with an idle curiosity, not a curiosity requiring questions. As long as she doesn't interfere with the playoffs.

Marge takes a break to visit her coffee shop friends. She sits and listens to how wonderful it will be to return to Montreal, to walk its fine streets, to sit in its fine parks.

Many years have passed since Marge visited the city of her adolescence. Closing her eyes as they talk, she imagines herself there, still young, still beautiful, still whole. Not the transparent outline she's become.

Yesterday, certain of her transparency, she tried to walk through the kitchen wall. She'd planned on reappearing next to Doug, had hoped to give him a good jolt, maybe even a small heart attack.

Doug yelled for her to keep the noise down.

Marge asks her companions about her fading, but they only laugh, assure her she's as concrete as anyone. Wouldn't that be wonderful, Marge tells herself.

When she returns from the coffee shop, before she resumes her cooking and cleaning, she pours herself a coffee mug of rye, careful not to clink the bottle, careful not to alert Doug. Then she adds only enough coffee for colour, and goes back to her work.

****

The freezer and the fridge are full. Even the house is clean, including the oven. As the playoffs wind down, there are fewer games. None today. Doug is at the mall with Rejean when Marge pulls the small suitcase with the shoulder strap down from the upper shelf of her closet. Laying it open on her bed, she inserts items selected from her wardrobe. She walks to the washroom, rummages through the cabinet and returns with a handful of bottles, nestling them in among her clothes. The zipper closes easily.

Marge walks to the front door, sets her bag on the floor and sticks one arm, then the other, through the sleeves of her jacket. Retrieving her bag, she opens the door and steps through to the porch, turning to lock the door carefully behind her. Finally, she places her key beneath the burlap mat that issues a faded welcome, and turns and walks away, careful not to look back.

I'm really sorry about last year

"I'm really sorry about last year," he said. "I didn't say anything, but you were my first and I had no idea how to handle it."

She forgave him and they slept together that night.

In the morning she wrapped her arms around his neck and kissed him. "Good morning, sleepy head."

He pressed his body against the wall as close as he could. Cursed that he was trapped. When she snuggled in more closely he used her motion to roll over her and land on the other side.

"God," he said. "I can't believe how late it is." He sat up, trying to look casual, unhurried. "The other's must be up."

"They can take care of themselves."

He rose and walked to the window. The sun gleamed unsympathetically off the deep blue of the lake. "I'm starving. What do you have for breakfast."

She sat and rubbed her eyes. Shrugged. "Whatever's in the fridge."

Three weeks later he was drifting, his boat tied to three others, when she arrived in another. No one had smokes but her. As she handed them out, he asked for one.

She looked away and shook her head. Then threw him one. "Fuck you," she said.

He caught the cigarette and sat down glumly and did not speak but took the matches when they were passed.

Treadmill

I open my eyes and the dream disintegrates. The soothing, sweet aroma of my mother's coffee and bacon is replaced by the stench of sweat and urine, of stale alcohol oozing from torn, wooden floor boards. Sunlight slashes through shredded window shade attempting to blind me, while outside misunderstood youths bash on a garbage bin chanting a perverse, unfamiliar rhyme. My head begins to pound in sympathetic unison.

The hangover is, as always, the old man's fault. His will is much stronger than mine.

I lift my head gingerly and look around the room. It's the same as all of the rooms I have had over the past few years. One set of shit-brown drawers, a broken mirror over a cracked and rusted sink, and the only paint that's not peeling is the graffiti.

FUCK U.

LIFE SUCKS. SO DOES ARLENE. A good Samaritan, or maybe Arlene herself, has gouged over the number with a ball point pen.

The thumping in my head is soon joined by a thumping against the wall. The couple next door is fucking. They're always fucking or fighting. Sometimes it's hard to tell the difference. And one usually leads to the other, locking them in an endless circle of fucking and fighting and fucking and fighting. I hear everything through the emancipated walls.

Sometimes I masturbate to the sounds of their confused and

angry sex. The woman's not half bad and I wouldn't mind giving her a try myself. I like the urgency, the desperation, in her voice when she comes.

She doesn't know I exist.

A painter used to live in their room. Blind in one eye, he painted bloated faces that critics thought were a clever comment on society, but that he said were simply a product of his lack of depth perception. Occasionally, he would sell a painting and buy a good bottle of Chivas or Johnny Walker Black and we would sit in his room and listen to Strauss, whom the painter said had written the most beautiful music ever. I thought he might have been right, but the old man could have cared less. He was only there for the booze. They took the painter away the night he set his canvasses on fire and I haven't heard of him since.

Before the painter there had been an older man who had lost his job, his home, and his family - in that order. Eventually, he lost the room next door as well. I still see him in the street every once in a while. He is always drunk and swears at himself and passers-by often and only the old man, not I, tries to speak with him.

I spot last night's bottle slumbering on the floor beside me. The old man reaches for it and I try to tell him no, to tell him it's too early and that I need to start the day fresh, but he ignores my protests. Reaches for the bottle, checks the dregs for butts, and then the harsh liquid washes over his lips and burns on his tongue, scorches my throat as he swallows.

When the bottle is empty, when the pounding in my head forces me to rise, I rinse my face in the sink. Leave the water running and piss in it through the slot in my jockey shorts. Realise I have to do more.

I put my ear to the door and listen. Open it a crack, step through and scurry to the toilet stuck in a cupboard at the end of the hall. Try to wipe the piss that's splattered across the seat, but the brown paper towel that serves as toilet paper absorbs nothing, only smears. I brush the piss onto the floor like dust. Squat and my bowels run loose and foul.

****

I lurch through the hotel entrance and the concrete slaps hard against my feet. Sunlight assaults my eyes, dashes me against the wall, dances on my eyelids like steel-toed fireworks.

I shade my wounded eyes, wait a moment, then open them slowly. Satisfied, I light a cigarette and wander unsteadily towards Queen Street where I know there will be something to occupy my day. I faintly recall doing the same thing as a student. The memory reminds me I haven't yet had enough to drink.

I pause before a familiar patio. It's cut off from the street by long rows of old, wooden fencing, the kind you see at the edge of country roads, lying hidden among the trees, broken, low and camouflaged by a coating of moss: a decaying sign of failed pastures.

The patio's full of students, laughing and drinking. I try to listen in, but can't make out what they're saying. Try to recall my own past conversations there.

Sex. Sooner or later every conversation turned to sex.

A few students glance in my direction, but look right through me. Most pay no attention at all. They're only interested in their world, only willing to leave it long enough to watch red and green-haired teenagers pass by.

I feel as though I no longer belong, even though this is my home - my street. When these students have gone, when they've forgotten the names of the friends they're sitting with and the things they talk about, I'll still be here. But for now, the patio - the city - has become their pasture, their world.

But it is ... it was ... mine.

An old habit resurfaces and I look for familiar faces. Recognise one. A classmate. Smile. Begin to wave, but the student dismisses me with a scratch of his nose, and I realise I can't possibly know this person. I've grown too old.

His age - the student's age - pisses the old man off.

"They're all so goddamn cocky. Who the hell do they think they are anyway?" His voice rises and people on the patio begin look in our direction.

I try to quiet him.

"What the hell are you looking at? Goddamn kids. Goddamn kids!"

A waiter turns toward us. The old man hunkers down into his best boxing stance, but I tell him to shut the fuck up and turn away. Continue my unsteady journey, knowing the old man will have to follow, his worn shoes shuffling faintly on the sidewalk beneath me.

In the transient reflections of store front windows I catch glimpses of the old man. I watch and try to make him stand taller, to make him look more dignified, but the effect is minimal. He remains an old man in a shabby jacket resurrected from a Salvation Army rack.

I stop and the old man's transparent image peers out from a window. Smiling mischievously, he removes the jacket made redundant by the mid-afternoon heat, and stuffs it in the nearest garbage bin.

Further along, we approach a street vendor hawking shiny cotton jackets with the names of rock groups on the backs. We recognise one: Def Leppard. They've played town recently. We've seen their posters. The appropriateness of the name makes me smile. I tell the old man Toothless Tigers would be even better and we chuckle discreetly. While we don't know the band's music, we do know that wearing their jacket will make us more noticeable - will make us stand out in a crowd. We'll be different. Maybe people will even think of us as eccentric.

We're tired of being chameleons, of being a part of the surrounding concrete - cracks in the sidewalk that people avoid without seeing. Step on a crack, break your mother's back. Give the poor dog a bone. Maybe throw him a quarter if you're feeling good.

I slip the jacket on. Too big, but I can wear a sweater underneath when the cold returns.

"Hey, Pops! You like the jacket?"

I nod to the young man.

"Twenty bucks and it's yours."

I search the old man's pockets frantically, but hopelessly.

"C'mon, Pops. Twenty bucks or take the thing off. I got other people who might want it."

I mumble an explanation as I remove the jacket.

"Sure. Sure. Pops. I do the same thing all the time." His eyes lock onto mine for a brief moment. "Listen, Pops. You find your money, you come back. I'll even let you have it for fifteen."

I retrace our steps, searching in vain through the trash bins for the old man's jacket, then sit on the sidewalk to rest. The old man raises my hand to a passer-by.

"Spare any change?"

****

The sun retreats behind the tall, concrete buildings and with the darkness comes the early autumn cold. As I walk I rub my shirt sleeves trying to warm my arms.

The old man's panhandling was quick and easy. In my hand I hold the benefits: a bottle in a brown paper bag. I smile, thinking I must be the perfect image for a sociology class. I imagine the professor at the front of the classroom, pointer in hand: "Now here's a fine example of a street person (he wouldn't call me a "man on the street"; no one cares what products or political parties I support). One of the city's thousands of homeless. Note the slow shuffle, the worn and torn clothes. Why, you can practically smell the dirt and grime of the city on him."

A homeless old man ...

I am ...

a homeless old man.

I raise the bottle to my lips and the liquid washes my throat taking my thoughts with it. The alcohol kills all germs - it disinfects and sanitises. As I lower the bottle, the thoughts dissipate and I hurry toward the hotel before they can resurface.

When we arrive Sarah's sitting on the sidewalk, her back against the building. Eyeing her tattered but warm overcoat, I mutter one final oath at the old man for losing his. At least, for now, we have a room.

Sarah speaks without looking up. "Can I stay here tonight?"

I tell her yes; she's the one person the old man rarely fights with.

"Got anything to drink?"

I show her the bottle. She stands and together we go upstairs.

In the room we share the bottle as we've shared a past - a way of life that we've rejected - or that's rejected us. Once Sarah had been a handsome young woman with potential. Won a high school public speaking contest at fourteen. But that was before they had conspired against her, before they had decided she was unworthy of their consideration and driven her from her home and family. They still watched her, still thwarted any attempts she made at happiness. She knew because she heard their whispers. For now she is, like the old man, simply a crumpled heap of foul clothing.

"Where've you been?"

Sarah reaches for the bottle as she answers. "Not far. The shelter. I needed food."

This hurts the old man. "I could've given you some."

"Yeah, sure. And what were you planning on using for money."

"I had some," he replies defiantly.

As Sarah returns the bottle, she examines my face. "It's not fair," she says. "We shouldn't be here."

I shrug. "I don't know. Maybe it's as good here as anywhere."

The bottle's nearly empty, leaving only a man and a woman sharing a dark and dirty room with the flies. Sarah rises and stands before me. Runs her hands through my hair. Draws my face gently into her breasts. I reach behind and pull her tight against me. We grope at each other in the dark, remove only the necessary clothes. Fall to the bed, where the sheet is crusty with semen and stale alcohol. As we make love, we don't kiss. Nor do we talk. And we're thankful for the darkness; it hides the old and dirty truth.

In the morning, when I awaken, Sarah's gone. I lie with my eyes closed and listen to the sounds of the street below. It's strangely quiet and I wonder what time it is, what day it is. In the distance, faintly, I hear church bells.

There are no dreams this morning, no images of a better time, only the steady hum of a city awakening - like a giant treadmill, and I am the rat. Stopping the hum would be as easy as stepping from the wheel, letting my joints stiffen and my bones wither in the dust that lies on the floor of my cage.

I sit up and look in the sliver of mirror above the sink. The old man stares back sadly and then reaches for the bottle.

Holes

A black hole has gravity so great that nothing can escape it, not even light. If you look at a black hole through a telescope for too long it will sap the life right out of you.

My brother told me these things. He had a telescope. If he caught me using it he'd push me roughly from his room. A telescope is a boy's toy, he said.

My husband has a telescope.

****

The moonlight bleeds through the trees and through the window, oozes onto the bed, and splotches his face which is looking up, always up. I rise and open the window. He closes it every night, winter and summer, before he climbs in beside me.

I've always loved to sleep in the cold, have always loved to bury myself deep in a hole in my goose down comforter.

He's allergic to feathers. Now we have an allergy-free comforter, but it's not the same. You can't dig a good hole in synthetics. I tested his allergy once, replaced the new comforter with my old, real one. He wasn't lying.

With the cool night air arrives the trickle of the stream that runs behind the farm house and the deep, foreign love song of the bull frogs. They remind me of the deep, low murmurs the Italian men would push towards my girlfriends and me in Europe after graduation. We ignored them as we'd been told to do. I can't ignore the bull frogs or their reminder that I'd once travelled, had once been the object of lustful thoughts in a language I didn't understand, still don't understand even though I've been in love many times.

He lies beside me and begins to snore in unison with the frogs. This new sound ends the memory. I am what I am. A forty-year-old mother of three with sagging breasts, scars from two Caesareans, and a husband who is growing as tired of me as I am of him. We've been married eighteen years.

She's in her early twenties, barely older than our eldest. A receptionist at his law firm. Not even a legal assistant. I could understand if he was at least able to talk with her. But then, he never wants to talk with me.

When we were first married he would talk. He'd tell me what his job would do for him, for us, but he never discussed his work. Perhaps I wasn't smart enough for him.

My degree was in political science, but I was more interested in political action than theory. That's what first drew him to me. It was also the first thing he criticized after we got married. Asked when I was going to grow out of it.

The pillow his head lies on is new. Qualofill. A play on quality. I look at his face and wonder if it breathes. His mouth. The pillow. Do they breathe - could they breathe - together, one through the other?

I saw them downtown together. It was on Saturday morning. He said he had some shopping to do. The usual, Canadian Tire kind of shopping. Saturday morning chores kind of shopping. Then he was to stop at the office for a few hours.

They were drinking coffee and eating croissants on the patio of a small restaurant. She was wearing spandex shorts and a t-shirt, Reebok trainers on her feet. There was a sports bag hanging from the back of her chair.

I haven't had a croissant in years. He says they're not good for us. Too much something. He's always watching our diets. He wants us to look like her.

I resisted the urge to confront them, to catch him in an undeniable situation. There was a time when I wouldn't have hesitated to do so.

His snoring is now out of sync with the bull frogs. They have a rhythm, a beat. He snores like he dances, slightly off. The only thing missing is the sly smile. He thinks he looks good on the dance floor.

The truth is - he does. I lied before. I was always happy to be seen dancing with him.

An Italian tried to kiss me when we were by ourselves for a moment. We were lagging behind the others who'd rounded the corner in front of us. He grabbed me and pushed me against the wall, tried to press his lips against mine. I turned my head away. He only wanted something to tell his friends.

Later, as we walked down the lane that led to our hotel, he looked across the water to an island we couldn't see. He told me this island had been his home, although he hadn't returned in many years. He looked so sad. I reached up and pulled his head towards mine, pressed my lips against his. I led him to the beach and made love to him. I knew there was no danger. Afterwards, he lay in my arms and continued to search for his island.

I told my friends what had happened.

Details, they said. We want details.

I get a Christmas card from one of them each year. It has a picture of her husband and herself surrounded by four well-dressed, smiling children. One child is holding a small dog in her lap. Inside is a photocopy of a letter that brings the reader up to date on the events of their lives over the past year.

This year the dog died. He was older than any of the children and would be sorely missed. They bought a new one two days later because the hole he left was too great to bear.

I am a hole, lying in bed beside him. I used to swallow him whole. He told me he would be lost without me, no longer whole. Now he's just lost. Doesn't know who he is anymore. He thought he did, but nothing is clear the way it used to be.

You can lay branches over a hole and trap a wild animal.

If you place sharpened sticks in the bottom of the hole, you can kill the animal.

hole (hol) 1. a hollow or hollowed-out place; a cavity 2. a small, dingy, squalid place 3. a prison cell 4. a flaw; fault; blemish; defect.

No longer whole.

In the moonlight I can see his pants neatly folded over the back of the chair. There are no crumpled clothes on the floor, no half-empty glasses of wine on the nightstand, only a television on its own table at the foot of the bed and a remote control by the clock radio with the exact time flashing in dull, red neon.

The alarm is set. He wants to be at the office early. Miss the traffic. Get a head start on the day's work load. No time to make love. Besides, the kids might come in.

He's forgotten we made those kids. He thinks they came with the Globe and Mail, like the Report on Business magazine. An extra-special treat. They can stay around for longer than the paper. These items have what they call longevity.

They expire in hospital waiting rooms.

The love song of the bull frog is gradually being replaced by the singing of birds. The open window has lowered the temperature in the bedroom by several degrees and I attempt to burrow into the allergy-free comforter. In doing so, I pull the comforter too far and expose his back to the cool air.

I begin to reach across his body carefully, trying not to waken him, reaching to replace the cover, but I stop myself. I retract my hand and use it to scrunch the comforter in front of my face, nestle my nose in to keep it warm, and pull on the comforter just a tiny bit more.

A Dense Garden

Alex tied the back of his cedar strip Peterborough tight against the dock, flipped the bumpers over the gunnel, and walked to the dirt road that ran past the head of the lake. He crossed the road to the store and stopped. Looked south to where the road climbed the hill and passed out of sight among the trees that blanketed the area as far as he could see. There was no sign of dust and the sun beat down hot upon his naked back.

Inside the store he returned Madame Millette's greeting and walked to the jars of candy near the cash register. Choose a few jujubes and two sticks of liquorice.

"Tu as un ami qui viens?" Madame asked.

"Oui. From where I used to live."

"C'est un bon temps pour venir. The weather is supposed to be good."

Alex smiled, walked out onto the porch letting the screen door swing shut behind with a loose wooden bang. Sat at the top of the stairs and popped a jujube into his mouth. Sucked on it rather than chewed while he watched the road.

The dust settled and the door of the bus swung open wide and Jake climbed down. The boys shook hands and then waited awkward and silent while the driver pulled Jake's bag out from the luggage compartment beneath the bus. Alex bent to scoop up the bag, but Jake grabbed at the handle and swung it up over his shoulder before he could reach it.

"Where to, Chief?"

Alex pointed across to the lake where the boat waited still snug against the dock.

Jake stood at the edge of the dock and admired the boat and engine. "Nothing better than an old Johnson," he said.

"You can say that again."

"Christ, they'll run forever. Thirty horsepower?"

"Eighteen."

"God, they were big back then."

"But so simple."

"Yeah. Simple and dependent." Jake settled on his haunches and ran his hand along the wood of the gunnel. "That's a beauty of a cedar strip."

"Dad and I stripped her down in the spring. Put a coat of fibreglass on the hull. Slows her down a bit, but at least she's solid and she runs smooth."

The boys climbed in and Alex pumped the bulb on the gas line twice, pulled the choke on, braced his left arm against the top of the engine and yanked the starter cord. The engine raced with the rich mixture and then the choke was off and Alex shifted into gear and they left the dock and the village and headed toward the open water. The boat glided slow and steady down the lake past well-spaced cottages and boathouses with open doors and they saw people lying on their docks and children playing on the beaches that separated one dock from the next.

"How far?"

"Four or five miles."

"Well, to hell with this." Jake pulled his shirt up over his head and spread his tanned arms and offered his chest to the warmth of the sun. "Ah, Christ. Now that feels good. What say we go for a swim before we get there?"

"But you're in jeans."

"Suits right here." Jake zipped open his bag and pulled out blue trunks. Swivelled to face the front of the boat and Alex looked off toward the shore as Jake tugged his jeans from each leg and pulled on his trunks.

"Ready," Jake said and Alex turned back on the handle until the engine cut out and they both stood up on the seats as the old cedar strip settled and glided to a halt.

Jake peered down into the water. "How is it?"

"Colder than yours. Lake's a lot deeper, but it's still pretty warm."

"Well, here goes nothing." Jake leaped high over the gunnel and sliced into the water. Alex followed before Jake's head broke the surface. When he came up Jake immediately splashed at him. "You jerk. This is freezing!"

"You'll get used to it. Are you a man or a mouse? Come on. Squeak up." The boys laughed at the old and familiar joke and a slice of the two years that had passed since Alex had moved to the city and they had last seen each other began to melt away.

They climbed back into the boat simultaneously from opposite sides to keep it on an even keel. Lay on their backs across the cedar seats. "You still hang out with Jimmy and Darren?"

"Not really," Jake replied. "They've turned into a couple of real assholes."

"What do you mean?"

"They're always stoned now. It's all they do."

"You can hardly blame them. What else is there to do there?"

"I don't seem to have a problem keeping myself amused."

"Aren't you Mr. Wonderful."

"Jesus," Jake said. "What's your problem?"

"I don't have a problem. You just don't have to sound so goddamn superior, that's all."

"Christ, I hardly said anything."

Alex squirmed on the bench to scratch his back and neither boy looked at the other. "What about drinking?"

"What about it?"

"I suppose you're never going to drink either?"

"Don't be ridiculous!" Jake raised himself onto his elbow. "Nothing better than a cold beer on a hot summer day. Dope's different." Then he smiled. "Only dopes smoke dope."

Alex lifted his head and looked at Jake and for one brief moment wanted to reach across the space between them and smash him in the face. He settled onto his back and closed his eyes against the sun. "All right," he said. "Just don't try and take away my beer."

"Don't anyone try to take away our beer," Jake said.

Alex wished they'd picked up some at the store. He pulled a pack of cigarettes from the pocket of a shirt that lay on the floorboards, shook one out and offered it to Jake. Jake shook his head.

"When did you start smoking?"

Alex shrugged. Lighted a match and drew in. Exhaled and threw the match over the side and listened to it land with a barely audible sizzle.

“There’s a dance at the clubhouse on Saturday night.”

"Are there a lot of good looking girls from the city here?"

"You better believe it." Alex said. "Way more than in Shawneeville!"

"Anywhere has more good looking girls than Shawneeville."

"You know why SHS has a concrete playground?" Alex asked. "To keep the girls from grazing." They both started laughing and then it was Jake's turn.

"You know why the girls at SHS have pockmarks all over their faces? From being poked with ten-foot poles." Alex was caught with a lung full of smoke and his laughter turned quickly into a coughing spasm.

"Have another cigarette, why don't you?"

"Christ," Alex said as his coughing subsided. "You turn into a goddamn prude or what?"

"At least I'm not filling my lungs with black shit."

"Screw you, you goddamned farmer boy."

"Screw you, too."

They turned from each other and gazed back up into the sky and then Alex sat up and started the engine. He watched the engine until Jake had raised himself to a seated position. "Ready?" He turned the handle full throttle and the nose of the boat leaped high into the air and then settled down as the it planed out and sliced through the water. Then he pulled the handle toward him and the boat went high on its port side until it felt as if they were ready to tip. Jake gave a loud whoop and smiled his approval as Alex pushed the handle far away from his body and the boat swung hard onto its starboard, the boys' heads skimming inches from the surface of the water made smooth by the pressure of the boat.

"She handles great," Alex yelled above the roar of the engine.

Jake nodded. "Can I try her?"

"Better not."

"Why not, for Christ's sake. You drove mine all the time."

"Yeah, but that was only a nine. Besides, my dad might not like it. Maybe after you've been here a few days."

"Let's get home," Jake said. He turned and stared out over the bow.

At the cottage Alex's mother had lunch ready. Hovered about as they ate. "It's so good to see you boys together again. Inseparable since you were just babies." They smiled sheepishly but didn't look up. Afterward, they laid on the dock and read and swam when they got hot and talked little and the sun passed quietly and slid beneath the tree line leaving the dock in shade.

"Should be about dinnertime for trout."

"I suppose so." Alex didn't like fishing. Too slow. Too dull. And he couldn't stand the smell or the taste of fish. He didn't mind reeling one in, though. The tug of war he had no chance of losing, unless the fish came off. And that didn't matter because mostly all you caught were scrappies and suckers who'd been around since the lake had been forced to go public by the government a decade earlier. Outside fisherman had brought all kinds of minnows in even though it was against the law and trout eggs were a favourite meal of most fish that were unfit for eating and now the trout were almost gone.

Jake didn't care. "Let's steal some of your dad's beer and just sit and enjoy the solitude."

They trolled where the lake plunged from twenty feet down to over one hundred and Jake landed two small keepers - frying pan specials, he called them - but Alex had not even a nibble. He traced his line's path as far as possible before it disappeared into the black, but there was nothing to see and then Jake was telling him how to jig his line so the fish would think his minnow was still alive.

"I know how to jiggle my line, for Christ's sake."

Jake kept looking out over the water. "Okay, Okay. I was just trying to help."

"So you caught two fish and all of a sudden you're mister goddamn fisherman. I'm the one who brought you to this spot. You've never even been on this lake before, so don't go trying to tell me how to fish it."

"Christ. I said I was just trying to help."

Alex finished his beer and placed it in the empty slot in the case and pulled out another. "You ready?"

Jake held his bottle up to see how much was left, nodded and tilted his head back. Let the last of the liquid flow free and easy down his open throat. "Labatt 50. That all your dad drinks?"

"All he's ever drank."

"I like Molson's. Give me an Ex anytime."

"There's nothing wrong with 50."

"No. There's nothing wrong with it. I'm just saying I prefer Ex. That's all."

Alex began to reel his line in. "Let's cast awhile."

He started the engine and let it run low and quiet while Jake finished reeling his line in, shifted into forward and gave the handle a quick twist. The boat shot forward, Jake just managing to maintain his balance, and raced across the dusk-smooth water. In Black Bay he cut the engine abruptly and again Jake fought to keep his balance.

"Jesus, man. You could warn me."

Alex pointed to a tree that had fallen along the shore and now laid half submerged. "There's a good spot for bass. Pass me the hoola hooper."

"This black one?"

Alex nodded and pulled his minnow from its hook. Threw it overboard and watched to see if something would strike while he freed the hook from its leader. Then he attached the hoola hooper and by the time he looked back, the minnow was gone. Probably just scrappies.

They fished and nothing bit and Alex hated being there.

"Do you remember that night?" Jake said.

"No."

"It was all your idea."

"No, it wasn't."

"Yes, it was. I remember. You told me that it really felt good and to do it to myself."

"I did not."

"Yes, you did. And then you came down and did it to me and then made me do it to you."

"It didn't mean anything."

"It was the worst thing I've ever done."

"For Christ's sake. It didn’t mean anything. We didn't even know what we were doing. We were only kids, goddamn it."

"It was the worst thing I ever did, and it was all your idea."

"You take that back." Alex pushed Jake off his seat to the floor of the boat. Leaped on top and sat across his chest pinning his arms with his legs. "You take that back, you bastard."

"It was the worst thing I ever did and it was all your idea," Jake said, angry spittle flying off his lips into Alex's face.

Alex hit him. Hard across the side of his head and again across his mouth and then Jake was struggling beneath him and crying out and there was blood running from his nose and down his upper lip and Alex kept him pinned until he calmed down and then slid off and returned to his seat.

From the bottom of the boat Jake glared at him. Wiped the blood from his mouth and looked at it. "You prick. You goddamned prick. I knew I shouldn't have come. I just want to get the hell out of here. But how am I supposed to tell your mother that? Shit. Two more weeks. Two more goddamn weeks of this. How the hell are we ever going to do it?"

Alex turned away from him, picked up his rod and cast toward shore. "As far as I'm concerned, you can leave whenever the hell you like." he said. Then he listened to the deep pounding of the blood flowing through his ears and barely heard Jake tell him to go to hell.

****

Alex and Jake were on the dock reading. Or Jake was reading. Alex was watching his older sister, Chloe, and Jocelyn, who lived in a cottage down the lake. The girls were lying on towels near the water and talking and Alex was watching the girls over the top of his book. He was watching their legs move as they shifted for comfort. And he was looking at the mound that rose between Jocelyn's legs as she lay on her back. The sun beat down hot on his own groin and he felt like he could barely contain himself. Wished he could stop time and whip out his prick and masturbate right there on the dock. With real girls instead of magazines. His gaze wandered from Jocelyn to his sister and he noted the smooth tautness of her stomach and how her breasts flattened out to the sides. He felt guilty for looking at her in that way and turned his eyes back to Jocelyn.

When he could no longer stand it he rose. Said he needed to pee and hurried up to the cottage where he climbed the stairs to his bedroom. Stood in the shadows just back from the window so that he could see the dock without being seen. Yanked his trunks down to his knees and began to stroke himself.

He watched Jocelyn smear tanning lotion on her legs and then Jake stood and dove into the lake and when he climbed up the ladder and stood with the water dripping from his slim body, Alex remembered the smoothness of him sliding through his hand so long ago. He knew that what he was thinking was wrong but he felt the pressure building inside and then he erupted into a tissue in a gush of guilt.

He returned to the dock and, without looking toward Jake, picked up his book. Then he listened to Chloe and Jocelyn discuss boys. He heard them mention Jake.

"What's with you?" he said. "Is boys all you think about?" He hadn't meant for the words to sound so harsh, but once started, his mouth seemed to operate without him. "Christ," he said to Chloe. "What are you? A slut? My sister the slut."

Chloe stared at him open mouthed. "Alex..."

"Well, that's what you are isn't it? I know you screwed Ricky."

"I never..."

"That's what he tells everyone, so it might as well be true."

"I've never heard a brother speak to a sister this way," Jocelyn said.

"Why not? If she can't control herself, why not?"

"What the hell...?" Jake was looking at him with disgusted stupefaction.

"Screw you," Alex said. "Screw you and screw everything."

He stormed back up to the cottage and threw himself onto his bed. Laid for what seemed a long time listening for footsteps, but there were none. After a while Alex forgot he'd wanted someone to follow him and listened to the birds in the trees outside his window and to the water lapping gently at the rocks along the shore and thought about who he would dance with on Saturday night.

who would have thought?

"Who would've thought," he said, "that I'd find the girl of my dreams in the middle of nowhere?"

He'd been engaged to the last girl of his dreams and they'd lived together with his twin brother until one night in the throes of passion she'd called out his brother's name. It hadn't taken long to pack his things and leave, but had left him with the problem of deciding where next to go. The mountains had seemed as good a place as any.

"I mean, can youse imagine? Out here. Stinking middle of nowheres. More bears than people. And she's here."

The girl of his dreams was indeed there. Seated across the table in the staff dining room. Looking as old as her sixteen years would let her. She'd arrived for the summer in a Mercedes with her parents who knew the owners of the lodge and who thought it would be a good idea for her to learn what it was to earn a living, but under the safety of a watchful eye.

He was a cook who planned not to stay short order forever. He'd actually planned on moving on by now, but he promised the girl of his dreams that he'd stick around until she left for school.

At first she'd let him hold her hand as they sat around a staff campfire. And then she let him kiss her. She was curious to see how this boy with bad grammar would kiss. It was no different really than any other boy's kiss until he tried to slip her the tongue. She resisted, pulling away quickly and his two front teeth fell to the ground between them. She was surprised more by his nonchalance than by her discovery.

"Fight," he explained.

She kissed him as little as possible afterward, which he respected as a by-product of her youth.

After she left he moved from job to job, each in a town that brought him closer to her in the city where he planned to arrive in time for Christmas. He phoned often but always seemed to get wrong numbers and cursed at the operators until they cut him off.

When he finally arrived at her address he found only a shopping mall and swore a blue streak at his own handwriting. Then he entered the mall and got a job at a hamburger joint and waited for her to come in.

The Crusted Wound

Hildred heard the knock on the front door from her bedroom. She checked the clock by the bed, then paused for one last look in the mirror. Raised her chin and ran her hand down across the fleshy ridges that hung beneath. She was a large woman, tall and corpulent, but her posture had not yet succumbed to the gravitational pressures of age.

She straightened the neck line of her dress where it ran across her more than ample bosom. Beneath the metal reinforced brassiere in which they were entrapped, her breasts stood proud and dangerous like nuclear warheads, daring any to challenge their will. Despite her own frequent declarations of helplessness, Hildred carried herself with the disciplined march of a drill sergeant, confident in the authority of her position, yet mindful that she must answer to a higher power. Had she believed in women in uniform, the Salvation Army might very well have benefited from counting her among their ranks.

Ignoring a second series of raps upon the door, Hildred lifted a small bottle of perfume from her boudoir and pumped the bulb decisively, aiming the nozzle first behind her ears, then across her chest. She replaced the bottle and marched to the front door, pausing before grasping the handle to glance behind where Ethel sat enraptured by the television. The volume was turned loud, so loud it would wake the dead, thought Hildred, but that was the only way the poor dear could hear it, even at a distance of not more than a yard. Hildred smiled sadly. Ethel had not been as fortunate as she when it came to avoiding the setbacks of advancing age.

Hildred took a deep breath and threw open the door in an exaggerated gesture of welcome. On the top stair stood her nephew. “Raymond. You’ve come,” she said, as though there had been some question.

Raymond smiled, appeared to teeter uncertain on the door jamb, then stepped forward in final acceptance for that which awaited him. “Hello, Aunt Hildred,” he said, kissing the cheek she proffered. “You smell very nice.”

Hildred smiled in spite of herself, pleased with his compliment. Although she wore perfume each and every day, there was only Ethel to notice. And, Hildred supposed, Manfred, but he more often than not possessed an odour of his own, although his was administered internally and was not the kind she cared to notice, and was certainly not the kind she would ever comment upon.

No, not since she had retired had there been much reason for perfume. At first, of course, there had been social gatherings to which Hildred was invited by her former colleagues at the high school, but these invitations had slowly dissipated. And then there was Ethel. She was in such a way now that it was hard to take her anywhere, and Manfred was useless when it came to caring for her. Always gallivanting about as if he was still forty.

“Don’t just stand there,” Hildred said. “Your Aunt Ethel’s in the parlour, and your uncle... Well, Lord only knows where he is. Always up to something.” She refrained from adding that the “something” Manfred was up to was almost certainly no good as she didn’t think it proper for one adult to criticise another before young people.

Raymond started. “He will be back though, won’t he?”

“Of course, Dear. Of course. I reminded him this morning you were coming. Though why you’re not staying with us, I’ll never understand. But then, you young people all seem to go your own way. For goodness sake, Ethel. Turn the television off. Look who’s here."

Ethel turned her head slowly, her eyes remaining on the television screen until the last possible second. "Darrel," she cried and raised her arms to accept his embrace. Then she held him by the shoulders, trapping him bent low at the waist. "Don't you look marvellous. Doesn't he just look marvellous, Hillie?"

Hildred cringed involuntarily at the name her sister used for her. It was fine for when they were alone, but in the company of others it was a different story.

Raymond smiled. Wormed his shoulders from her grip. "Thanks, Aunt Ethel. You look great yourself."

Hildred shook her head in disgust. "For pity's sake, Ethel," she shouted. "It's not Darrel. It's Raymond."

Ethel peered more closely at him. "You look just like your father. Doesn't he look just like his father, Hillie? You look just like your father. How is he?"

Raymond looked to Hildred to take his cue, but she continued to punch buttons on the remote until the television screen went black. "There," she said at last. "That's better. He's dead, Ethel. Darrel's been dead for almost fifteen years." She turned back to Raymond. "Look what we got especially for you," which wasn't technically correct, for the chewy candies she held out for Raymond had been bought some time ago, perhaps even for his last visit. No one else ate them. Small white lies were perfectly acceptable if they helped to preserve someone's feelings, Hildred thought. "Your favourite," she said.

Raymond took the bowl of candies and placed it on the coffee table. "Great. I'll have one later."

"Go on, Raymond," Hildred said. "Treat yourself. Dinner won't be for a while yet."

Raymond lifted a candy dutifully from the bowl. Removed the

wrapper and gestured with it in a kind of toast to both women. Popped the candy in his mouth and began chewing. “Delicious,” he said.

“Did he suffer?”

“Did who suffer, Ethel? The candy?”

“Darrel. Did Darrel suffer?”

“No, Aunt Ethel. He died in his sleep.”

“Oh. That’s nice. It must be terrible to suffer your last few minutes on earth. Although I suppose it might help you get into heaven. Suffer unto me the little children and all.”

“Are you going to tell us what brings you to Ottawa?” Hildred said, doing her best to ignore her sister. “Surely you didn’t come all this way just to visit three old coots.”

Raymond nodded as he swallowed the last of his candy. “There’s been some trouble with the ministry recently,” he said. “Like always, that means more time wasted in meetings.”

Ah yes, Hildred thought. The ministry. There was always something with the ministry. If Raymond hadn’t been her own brother’s son, she was sure she would dislike him simply on principle.

“What about the minister?” Ethel said.

“There’s nothing about a minister, Dear. He said ‘ministry’. You remember, Raymond is a civil servant.” Hildred said civil as though it left an unpleasant aftertaste in her mouth. She thought of how disappointed her brother would have been. Raymond, a trained engineer who should have been following his father’s footsteps, wasting his talents deceiving the people. That’s what he would have said, all right. Maybe not in those exact words, but Hildred knew that was what he would have meant.

“Your Uncle Bill was a minister,” Ethel said.

"Yes, I know."

"Lovely man, your uncle. Wasn't he a lovely man, Hillie? Had a beautiful little church in a town not too far from here, I think. Isn't that right, Hillie?"

"Yes, Dear. Not too far from here. So I gather this means you'll be staying in the public sector then."

Raymond smiled. "It's been over ten years, Aunt Hildred. And yes, I'll stay. Same as you did."

Hildred returned his smile with as much insincerity as she thought would go unnoticed. "Same as me. Yes. I guess that's right." In her heart Hildred knew it was the farthest thing from the truth. It was one thing to dedicate your life to educating the nation's youth. It was another to leach off them.

In some ways, Raymond reminded Hildred of a student she'd taught many years earlier. Not an overtly unpleasant boy. Bright. But too big for his britches. And insolence was one thing Hildred would not stand for. What was his name? she wondered. What was his name? "Jeremy Bond."

"Who's that."

"Who's who?"

"Jeremy Bond. You just said that name."

"Did I?" Hildred was a little flustered. She hadn't realised she'd spoken the name aloud. She recovered quickly and looked directly at Raymond. "He was a student of mine," she said. "Very smart, but also very cheeky."

"He'd do well in politics then."

"He was forever late with his work. One semester, he handed in three late assignments in the same course. I wanted to fail him, on those papers at the very least, but the fools in the office thought that because he was involved in a number of extra-curricular activities, he was the kind of boy who would be successful later in life. Naturally, I insisted that no punishment would only encourage his lax behaviour. If you let them get away with it at that age, they'll never grow out of it. But, they decided against it. How can you be a productive member of a civilised society if you have no discipline?" She gave Raymond her sternest look when she said this, but he seemed to take no notice.

"I'm sure he's doing just fine if he was lucky enough to have you for a teacher, Aunt Hildred."

Hildred disliked condescension almost as much as she disliked laxness. "That's very kind of you to say, but I think you're missing the point. The point is ..."

"Do you think Uncle Manfred will be back soon?" Raymond rose and walked to the window.

"Yes, Dear. I'm sure he will. Now the point I was trying to make was..."

"Did he say where he went?"

"No. He never does. The point is," she said, determined not to be put off again, "Jeremy was a product of no discipline. Like your uncle." There. She'd said it. She couldn't make it any plainer than that without pointing fingers, now could she?

Raymond nodded his head, as though considering her message, while he looked at a group of photos spread across the window ledge. Each was taken out-of-doors. People standing dutifully at loose attention. Painful smiles held too long. Many of those pictured were probably dead now. They were old when the photos were taken. And in each the photographer had centred the faces so their heads appeared to float halfway between the bottom and the top of the photo in a sky of drifting clouds, as though their journey toward heaven had already begun. There was one face that was noticeably missing.

"Do you mean Manfred," Raymond said, "or Charlie?"

A look of surprise left Hildred's face as quickly as it arrived. "When your Uncle Charles was with us," she said, as though he were now dead, "he proved himself to be what I should have realised he was the first time I met him: an undisciplined heel. Not a shred of decency. How else can you explain one human being treating another in that fashion? Fortunately, I am a strong enough woman to deal with man's fragile loyalties."

"Did you ever hear from him again? After it was all over."

Hildred thought for a moment. Her nephew's questions were anything but proper. Bordering on impertinence actually. "Charles wrote once. To ask for a photo album he'd left behind. I told him it had been discarded."

"And had it?"

"Had it what?"

"Been discarded."

"Certainly. What possible use could I have for his old photos? The man had no discipline. No discipline leads to chaos." Just then the door to the apartment swung open and laughter came tumbling in.

Hildred swivelled to glare at the doorway where Manfred now stood with a woman before him, his hand in the small of her back. "You've brought someone with you," Hildred said through an emancipated smile. It was an accusation more than an observation.

The woman responded with a small belch that escaped her startled lips. She raised her hand quickly as if to catch it, then giggled. "I wonder where that was hiding," she said.

Manfred laughed. "No sense in keeping it bottled up inside," he said, with a soft swipe at her rump. "And to answer your question, my dear sister: Yes. I have brought someone home with me. Someone to help celebrate," he bowed in Raymond's direction, "our dear nephew's visit." Then he raised the hand of his friend and again tipped forward at the waist. “May I present, Chantel de la Forêt.”

His companion laughed and waved away his formality. “You just call me Chantal. La Forêt is the bar we meet in.”

Raymond’s uncle left her side and bounded forward to pump his nephew’s hand solidly. “Good to see you, my boy. I trust you had a pleasant trip. Has no one offered you a drink? Hildred. Why haven’t you offered the boy a drink?”

“Isn’t it rather early?”

“Don’t be ridiculous. What’s your poison, Ray?”

“Don’t tell me we have mice again,” Ethel said.

****

Dinner was not what Hildred had planned. Her brother’s compulsion to turn everything into a joke was beginning to wear thin. And there was his guest, who had to be fifteen years his junior if a day. One thing was certain: she was not from Ottawa.

“Un petit village,” Chantal said. “Mostly French. North of Kapaskasing. No one has ever heard of it.”

“You are probably right,” Hildred said. “I barely know where Kapaskasing is.” As she spoke her eyes turned to Manfred and Raymond. It was obvious they were drinking far too much. After she had gone through all the trouble of preparing a beautiful pork roast with the little potatoes she was certain Raymond loved, he had barely touched a forkful or uttered one word of thanks. His toast to the chefs may have been enough for her feeble-minded sister, who had, in all truth, very little to do with preparing dinner, but Hildred felt a little more gratitude would not have been unwarranted. But no, the wine Manfred kept pouring seemed more to their nephew’s liking, as did Manfred’s company now that she thought about it. The ingratitude of the young was something she had experienced as a teacher but that she would never understand, and would certainly never condone. She had been raised to say thank you and to pay proper tribute to extra effort, and since her brothers had been raised in the same house as her, they should know better, and so should their sons.

Raymond and Manfred broke into yet another good round of laughter. Hildred gave them a stern look of reproach. She hadn't caught what was said, and so was unsure why they were laughing, but the chances were very good that it was something off colour. She turned away in a subtle display of disapproval.

Beside Hildred, Ethel bobbed in sleep. As her head tilted forward, her shoulders collapsed and then jerked upright willed erect by an inner force that came from beyond the conscious. The resulting tug of war gave her the motion of a snore without the accompanying soundtrack.

Hildred shook Ethel's elbow lightly. Ethel's eye's slapped open. She looked around as if surprised by unfamiliar surroundings. "You were asleep," Hildred said.

"Did I miss anything?"

"You didn't miss anything," Manfred said. "For Christ's sake, Hildred. Why don't you leave her sleep?"

"No, that's all right. I wouldn't want to miss anything." Ethel smiled at her nephew.

"Has everyone had enough?" Hildred looked around the table. When her gaze met Manfred's, she gave him a stiff nod.

"What the hell is that supposed to mean?"

"What is what supposed to mean?" Hildred was embarrassed, but not surprised, by her brother's outward insensitivity.

"That little nod you just gave me. What do you think I'm talking about?"

"I'm sure I don't know what you're talking about. But now that you mention it, I could use some help in the kitchen."

"I could help you," Chantal said.

"No," Hildred said. "You stay." She realised she had spoken in the same tone she had used with Jock, her Scottish terrier, when he had misbehaved. But then, sometimes it was best to keep directions short and simple. To avoid confusion.

"Here we go again," Manfred said, standing to follow his sister through the swinging door to the kitchen.

"Here goes what again?" Hildred said as soon as the door swung closed.

"This. You. Can't stand to see people having a little fun. What the hell are you so afraid of, Hillie?"

Hildred knew he'd used the short version, the improper version, of her name simply to get her goat, but she was not about to rise to the bait. "I am not afraid of anything. Some of us choose to take our responsibilities seriously. Lord knows what would happen to the world if we didn't. The slack certainly would not be taken up by the likes of you."

"And just what responsibilities would you be referring to?"

"Keeping this house in order for one thing. Who do you think cleans? Who do you think prepares all of your meals?" Hildred could feel the blood rising to her face, but she would not allow herself to lose control. No matter what her brother did, she would not give him that.

"You do. And it is much appreciated. But the apartment is clean, and dinner is over. Lighten up for Christ's sake. We have guests, and this can be done later. Are you coming?" Manfred held open the door, then shrugged at her silence. "Suit yourself."

Music. We need music, Hildred heard him say as the door swung shut behind him. She stood for a time in the kitchen, her arms dangling down into the sink. The water ran, but she had not yet placed the stopper in the drain. She listened to Manfred shout out names as he shuffled through his album collection. “There is nothing,” Manfred said, “like the sounds of the big bands.” Hildred could picture him stacking albums on the turntable pin. The flicker of a switch brought scratched, uneven music.

Hildred heard Raymond say he would move the table, and then the shuffle of feet as people began to dance.

She turned off the tap and walked to the door and pushed it open. Manfred had Chantal in mid-twirl. Raymond was gesturing for Ethel to join him. She laughed but declined with a wave of her hand and a shake of her head. Reached for her wine glass.

“My goodness. Have you all lost your senses?” Hildred stood holding the door to the kitchen open, a dish towel draped across her shoulder.

“Hildred,” Manfred cried out. “Come dance, my dear sister. Grab your aunt, my boy.”

Raymond looked to Hildred, raised his eyebrows in hesitant invitation. By her look he knew the answer. He collapsed into a chair as she turned and the door swung shut behind her.

Hildred filled the sink and began to wash the dishes.

“You should have danced.” His presence did not surprise her. She glanced at Charles, but made no reply. You used to dance. Do you remember the Blue Note? You were my Isadora. He reached out to her, but did not touch her. You weren’t like this ... before.

“We were going to have children before,” Hildred said. “That’s why we got married. That’s what God wants married people to do.”

We got married because we were in love. I didn’t give a damn about what God wanted. I wanted you.

“It was no use,” she said. “I couldn’t give you what you wanted.”

You never asked me what I wanted. And even when I told you, you wouldn't listen.

"I don't expect you to understand. You didn't have it inside you. You have no idea what that was like. To lose something that relies only on you for its very existence. To fail it."

I relied on you for my very existence.

"I couldn't do it again. I couldn't risk another failure. You had to leave." Hildred looked up from the sink but she was alone in the kitchen.

A glass slipped from her hands and crashed to the floor. Raymond called to her.

"Everything's fine," Hildred said, steadying her voice as best she could. She dried her hands on the tea towel and left the rest of the dishes to soak in the sink.

The couple stopped dancing. "What are you doing?" Manfred said.

"Ethel and I are going to bed. And if you have any sense at all, you'll do the same." Without waiting for a reply, Hildred turned and disappeared down the hallway with the bewildered Ethel in tow.

As she came out of Ethel's room to go to her own, Hildred stopped. She could hear her brother and Raymond speaking. "She can't stand to see people enjoying themselves and wouldn't miss a chance to ruin it for the world," Manfred said.

"You're too harsh on her."

"Do you think so? I can't say I agree, my boy. Au contraire, I think I'm too easy."

****

Dressed in her night-gown, with only the bedside lamp for light, Hildred pulled a chair into her closet and retrieved a black book from the uppermost shelf. She carried it to her bed, sat and turned back the cover. **This Photo Album Belongs to** Charles John Parker. Hildred ran her fingers across the letters. Traced the curves of each elaborate shape that made up the name. Then, without looking at the photos that lay waiting inside, she lay on her side with her cheek against the page. She wanted to cry, but no tears would come.

Streetcars and Other Vehicles

one: BATHING

The sounds of others rising, talking, exchanging insults and profanities, cause Michael to open his eyes. He's lain awake for some time. Long enough to hear the man three beds down making his way back from the bed of another. Slipping almost silently into his own. Long enough to hear the man's sigh of satisfaction as he finally relaxed his body and relaxed his lungs and allowed himself to sleep. Long enough to recognise the difference between those sighs of release and the ones that had occurred in the darkness before.

Michael had been tempted to open his eyes, to watch the man's wilted erection and naked buttocks glide across the space at the foot of his bed. Even if the man had caught Michael looking he wouldn't have been worried. Everyone knows Michael's crazy. Everyone knows he understands nothing. Michael doesn't speak to them. He doesn't trust them.

And then someone is shouting at Michael. Hey, Michael. Time to get up for work. And there's laughter.

Michael's eyes remain open but he makes no response, stares hard at the folds in the sheet scrunched before his face by his withered fists.

A hand shakes his foot on its way to the showers. C'mon, Mikey. The world's awaiting.

Michael moves the sheet and watches a man's back roll away from him, rocking side to side like a boat riding ocean waves. Bodies swirl in and out of his vision, naked, half-dressed, unshaven, wet hair, toothbrushes protruding. A bottle hangs from one hand, is grabbed by another and disappears, returns and disappears again.

Michael waits for the traffic to subside, for uninterrupted space, and then rises. Eyes to the floor, he makes his way to the washroom, avoids feet in his path. Empties his bladder behind the small metal door, latch closed. Reaches forward and watches the water swirl and disappear. Waits for the fresh water to come. Reaches down and feels it run through his fingers. Grabs a handful and lets it trickle back into the bowl. Grabs another handful and throws it on his face, rubs it around vigorously. Up his cheeks, follows it down his chest and scoops what he can to the back of his neck. Feels it trickle down his spine to the small of his back.

Then someone is banging on the metal door.

You all right in there, Mikey? Fuck me, man. He's washing in the fucking shitter again. Michael! Open the fucking door! Someone go get Al. Tell him Mikey's in the can again. Jesus Christ!

two: LEASHES

The streetcar shudders to a screeching halt. Passengers crush against the windows and doors trying to peer outside to where a small crowd has instantly formed. Try to open the doors, but they won't budge.

Tell the driver to open the doors, someone says, but the driver's disappeared.

An anonymous hand reaches for a large red button near the steering wheel. Instantly, all doors on the streetcar swing open and a stream of legs and torsos explode from the vehicle's confines and flow toward the front of the vehicle. The promise of disaster is all too enticing.

At first, the passengers see only the back of an old man seated so close to the wheels it appears he's the victim. But the angle at which he sits is wrong. As the passengers press closer, over his shoulder they see the dog.

The dog's head is lying on the old man's thighs. His hind legs are severed near the hips and everyone instantly recognises death. The dog makes no sound, but its eyes are open, staring up into those of the old man as he strokes its neck and shoulders.

Oh, the poor thing, one passenger says. I hate when an animal gets hurt like that. They don't understand it's not their fault. They think they're being punished.

Goddamn, says another. I'm going to be late for a meeting. What's the stupid thing doing out loose on the street anyway? It's rush hour, for Christ's sake!

Don't be so heartless. We have to wait until the thing dies. Or at least until they can move it.

A police officer squeezes through the crowd and crouches beside the old man. They speak, but too quietly for the passengers to hear. Then the officer stands and speaks with the driver. He has his notebook out and is writing as the driver speaks. The driver says something with a wave of his hand and both men smile.

Behind them, the old man cradles the dog in his arms, speaking in a voice low and unwavering, and for the first time the passengers look at him. He's wearing a long ragged overcoat and the shoes on his feet, which protrude out from beneath the dog, are worn through in several spots. His face is dark and weathered and looks like the pictures of native Indians that many of the passengers have seen before.

Christ, says the passenger who's late for his meeting. Wouldn't you know it belongs to a goddamn Indian. No wonder it hasn't got a leash.

three: THE COAT

Jasper walks up the stairs and through the entrance of the station. No one stands near as he waits for an officer at the front desk to address him.

What can I do for you, pops?

My buddy Tinker. Think he’s dead. Jasper hopes the officer won’t notice the bulge caused by the bottle in the left top pocket of his overshirt.

Well, that's too bad, but what do you want me to do about it?

Don't know. Gotta do something with his body, don't ya?

Where exactly is this body?

In an alley a couple of blocks away. Thought he was just sleeping. Tried to wake him up, but he wouldn't.

When did you find him?

Twenty minutes ago. Came straight here.

The officer points to the far wall. Take a seat on the bench. Someone will be with you in a minute.

In the cruiser, the officer in the passenger seat turns and speaks to Jasper through the metal wire fencing that separates them. Jesus, Jasper. Don't you have any place you can take a shower?

When I stay at Sally Ann's sometimes I do. And when I was in the hospital, took one. Turn there.

And when was that? Last year?

A couple of months ago, suppose. Couple of your buddies found me. Sick as a dog I was. Jasper smiles at the officer. The doc wanted to know if I'd been drinking anti-freeze.

And were you?

Naw. Chinky Dinky.

Is that what you got in your pocket now?

Not gonna take it, are you?

The cop shakes his head. No. Don’t worry about it.

Jasper points to an alley on their left. In there. Behind the dumpster.

The three men stand in a semi-circle around the body, which is curled up in the foetal position. The cop who’d spoken in the car kneels down and checks for a pulse. Gives the body a soft push. He's dead all right. Getting pretty stiff. He stands and speaks to the other cop. You better call the morgue. I'll get what I can out of Jasper.

Can I have his coat? Jasper asks as the cop begins his routine.

four: LATE MORNING SUN

The old man's sitting near the back of the streetcar. Legs splayed into the centre of the aisle, making it difficult for anyone to pass. Overcoat's open and his untucked shirt is missing buttons, leaving a fleshy, hairy mass exposed to the sight of strangers. The strangers from whom he acquires most of whatever he has. A couple of dollars, a cigarette or two. Sometimes, if he's lucky, they buy him a drink in a local watering hole.

The old man has company today, sitting one row back and across the aisle. Younger, but like him, she looks worn.

He speaks loudly to his companion, including the rest of the passengers in his audience so as not to be rude. A couple of more blocks, he tells her. Then we can drink. Smiles an invitation to everyone.

Good, she replies, laughing. I so damn tirsty I tink my tongue grow big an' choke me.

They've been in his room most of the morning. Drinking the sherry they couldn't finish the night before. Passed out early groping each other through the layers of clothing they wear each day. The odours seeping from their bodies going unnoticed, like the stench of the shits they take in the tiny cupboard at the end of the hall where the toilet sits on its pedestal of ill-aimed urine and paper and cigarette butts.

But the sherry's gone and the Manor's open and they have money from a drunk she gave a blowjob to the night before in the recessed doorway of a neighbourhood pawn shop. The old man had waited dutifully across the street, watching as her head bobbed in and out, in and out of the shadows. Watching as he listened to the quiet laughter of sidewalk traffic. Watching as his left hand stroked his own erection feverishly until he erupted inside his pants with a grunt of satisfaction.

That was some blowjob you gave last night, he says.

Dat some ol' fart, she replies with a smile. Take damn near forever to come, she tells the other passengers. They laugh and she laughs and the old man laughs. They're only a couple of stops away from the tavern and the old man and the woman feel good knowing their first cold beer of the day is near.

You're a damn fine woman, Lil, the old man tells her. I can't imagine it taking very long for anyone.

Lil blushes at the compliment. Ah, go on, she says. You being silly. But her smile betrays her pleasure.

A young couple in black biker jackets are sitting in front of Lil and the girl swings 'round to face her. What's your secret, Lil? she asks, nudging her friend in the ribs.

Dere ain't no secret I don't know, Lil answers with a laugh. Ain't dat right, Barney? Get to be are age, an' dere ain't no secrets left.

Barney nods in agreement, then shrugs. Except maybe how to get rich.

Lil agrees with another raspy laugh. Yeah, she says. Except maybe dat. But we ain't doing so bad. We going out, ain't we?

By now the streetcar has reached their stop and Barney motions to Lil. Let's go, he says.

Goddamn right, Lil says. She looks around at the other passengers. Jus 'cos we pay for dis ride, don' mean we gotta take 'er to da end 'a da line.

They rise and when the doors swing open Lil shoves Barney roughly from the steps. He stumbles to the sidewalk and she laughs. He don't walk as good as he talk, do he? she says. Laughs again and clambers down behind him.

Through the windows the passengers watch as Lil and Barney push and shove their way through the door of the Manor and their shapes disappear from the late morning sun.

five: NEXT TIME

The first bottle crashes on the back of the door above Lloyd's arms which are wrapped around his head protectively. The second strikes his head just below his right hand with a thick, gooey thud. Lloyd slumps against the door. His body sags slowly to the floor in time with the blood which is trickling down his face.

Irma stands over him, hands mercifully empty. You fucking bastard! she says. What the hell you think I come here for? You fucking bastard!

Later, the policeman with his foot propped up on the sole chair in the room, makes one last mark in his notebook. He turns to where Irma is kneeling with Lloyd's head cradled against her breasts.

You can't keep doing this. We just can't keep coming here. The next time we're going to have to pull you in.

That's okay, Irma tells him. There ain't gonna be no next time. Ain't that right, Lloyd. We ain't gonna fight no more.

Lloyd looks up blankly at the officer. He wants desperately to be out of this woman's arms and to get a drink. Instead he simply nods.

Well, just see that there isn't. The officer moves toward the door his partner is holding open. In the hall he shrugs. What are we supposed to do with them? They're so fucking nuts. Sometimes I think it'd be best if they just killed each other.

six: AGAINST THE WIND

The cold December breeze whips her hair into a tangled mass and slices her worn, pock-marked features. Causes her dull, bored eyes to peer contempt. Her thumb is extended. An invitation, not a request.

Her face is clownish, her smile painted the deep red of her dress. It's the smile she wore as she packed her little one off to day-care. The smile she used to kiss him goodbye on the steps of the house where he'll wait for her return.

And she will return, her perfume barely strong enough to cover the scent of cheap cologne and semen, barely strong enough to cover the smell of the liquor she drinks all day in a vain attempt to numb.

She's old, too old for the oldest profession. She used to work downtown, used to make a good living doing what she knows best. Doing the only thing she knows. But now there are only the few faithful regulars who can't afford the downtown girls, who can't afford a hotel room or gas for their cars. The unemployed who seek a few moments of escape from the bills and the crying children who need to be fed. The aged who treat themselves to a moment of youth when their pension cheques arrive. Who seek reassurance that they're still alive. Reassurance that they can still function as human beings when the rest of the world has chosen to ignore their existence.

It's early and she has yet to turn her first trick of the day. Her makeup's still in place and she's still sober. Sober enough to despise what she's about to do. Sober enough to despise the drivers who pass by without giving her the chance to do it.

She reaches into her purse and pulls out a small plastic flask. She remembers when it used to be silver, a symbol of better times that has long since been sold. She unscrews the top, raises it to her lips and takes a large sip of the clear liquid inside. Closes her eyes and feels it burn against the lining of her empty stomach.

She remembers when she was the choicest on the street, when even her pimp would make love to her. She hasn't seen him in almost six years. Then she wouldn't have been able to work without him - or another - telling her where to stand and when to stand there. Now, no one cares where she stands. Not even the cops.

Commuters on a passing street car smile at the sight of her. Some with unsympathetic humour, others with disguised and embarrassed lust. But she takes no notice - no notice of the indifferent machine as it rolls by, or of the passengers whose stares intrude upon her world.

After the streetcar has passed, the commuters search for the next point of interest and forget the wounded woman with her thumb raised defiantly, her eyes slitted blind against the wind.

seven: TO THE STREET

The drunk climbs on and hands the driver his transfer.

Keep it, the driver tells him. They check them on this line. Fifty-five bucks if it's no good.

Right. I knew that, the drunk responds with a nod of his head. His eyes remain vaguely focused in the direction of the paper in his hand. Giving his head a shake, his body shudders into motion and he takes a seat several rows behind the driver. Swivels around to examine his surroundings. Seeing few other passengers, he moves in a crouch to the seat closest to the driver.

They been experimenting with animals again, he says.

Uh huh, replies the driver.

Yeah. For shit that ain't even needed. The drunk shakes his head in obvious disgust. Wouldn't be so bad if it was for shit we needed, but it ain't.

That so, the driver says.

Yeah, says the drunk. Animals shouldn't be killed, but they are less important than people. He turns toward the back of the streetcar, includes the other passengers with a sweep of his hand. Everyone on this streetcar, he cries out, is more important than animals. Our mothers made us that way. He nods his head firmly.

The driver tells him to keep his voice down and the drunk slumps back in his chair and fumbles to fetch a half-smoked cigarette from his coat pocket. The driver glances at the drunk's hand. Don't light that, buddy. Can't smoke on public transportation.

The drunk looks at the cigarette in his hand, as though he's unsure how it got there. Yeah, he says, looking up at the faces in the streetcar now turned toward him. He waves the cigarette in the air. I knew that, he tells the faces with a smile.

He settles back sideways in his chair, his arm resting on the back, and peers toward the rear of the vehicle. Watches a man climb down at the next stop.

Did you hear that guy talking his head off at the back? the drunk asks the driver.

The driver shrugs.

Must be in love, the drunk says. I was in love once. Well, more than once, he laughs, but once for real.

That so, says the driver.

Yeah. The drunk is nodding his head as he remembers her. Lives in California. Haven't seen her in almost ten years. Maybe more.

Uh huh, the driver says.

Bet she don't even know I'm still alive. Probably don't even remember me, the drunk tells him. Love sucks. You ever been in love? he asks.

Nope, answers the driver.

Yeah, says the drunk. You're lucky. Don't ever fall in love.

Sherbourne, the driver calls out.

Oh, says the drunk. That's me. He rises and stands at the top of the stairs waiting for the streetcar to stop. As he reaches the bottom stair he turns back toward the driver. Beware of bumps, he tells him, and then takes his coat and his smell and his half-smoked cigarette to the street.

eight: EACH TIME IT OPENS

He enters the all night coffee and doughnut shop and walks directly to three girls camped at the counter. Wants to know if one of them is free.

The girls turn their heads slowly. Look over their shoulders to give him the once over, backs still turned toward him.

He's dressed in black from head to toe. Oil-black jeans, torn. Black tee-shirt stretched over a bloated belly. Not quite long enough to contain the rolls of hairy, pucker-white flesh. From beneath his baseball cap run greasy smears of long, brown hair. His face has two days' stubble sprouting like patches of weeds among a bed of acne scars and pockmarks.

The girls immediately dismiss his presence and his stench - one mumbles something about regret that he can't make out - and he is forgotten as quickly as their last trick.

He's left staring at their backs, unsure of his next move. He hadn't anticipated being turned down. His eyes dart about the coffee shop, then he looks down at his feet, embarrassed, a child reprimanded in public.

Just then a thin, dark girl slithers out of the washroom, teeters on her high heels for a brief second, then approaches the counter. The man spots her. What about you? he asks.

What about me what?

Are you free?

The girl focuses on him, gives her head a barely perceptible shake as the initial rush from the hit in the washroom wears off.

Maybe, she tells him. I gotta check something first. Meet me here in five. She straightens herself and walks out the door.

Two women at a nearby table have halted their conversation

to watch. They tisk pitifully and then the blond in the white dress with enormous breasts calls to the man. Jerry. Over here. Her voice is deep. A man's voice.

Relieved, Jerry moves to sit beside the blond. The blond twirls one of her red, dangling earrings that match her lipstick as she asks how Jerry is doing.

Like shit, Jerry says, What else?

Ain't it the truth, says the blond. And then they're talking about crap that doesn't matter to any of them but fills the space between sips of coffee and drags on their cigarettes and Jerry keeps his eye on the door and dies a little bit each time it opens.

Considered a Virtue

A mosquito hovered in the weak circle of light thrown by the torch onto the wall of the outhouse, and then all was black. Harry cursed the batteries. Banged the torch against the wall.

Nothing.

He cursed himself for being unable to wait until morning. Pushed frantically down on his bowels. Did his business quickly and wiped, half-standing. In the dark, he never knew what creatures might emerge from the depths below his naked buttocks.

The door banged shut behind him and he hurried toward light. Toward the noise of his parents' party still in full swing. As he approached the cottage he was halted by the sight of two figures caught in the dim light cast from a bedroom window.

From his spot in the darkness he could see a woman, her back pressed against a tree. She had her legs wrapped around a man's waist, ankles locked, and her arms clung about his neck. The man, the woman's buttocks cupped in the palms of his hands, was hurling his body into hers with such a force Harry thought he would crush her. Above the music he could hear their desperate gasps for air. Could hear their quick guttural curses.

With a final heave, the man stopped. Their bodies tensed, then slowly settled loose and tired. The woman's ankles unlocked and her legs slid from the man's waist to the ground and light squeezed between their silhouettes.

Lifting her arms from the man's shoulders, the woman bent to retrieve something from the ground. Spoke and laughed at the man's reply as she slipped her legs through the holes of her bikini bottoms. She straightened her skirt, the type all the cottage women wore over their bathing suits, leaned and gave the man a quick kiss, his groin a final squeeze, before she strode toward the cottage.

The man watched her leave, lighted a cigarette and leaned against the tree. Harry stood still and quiet. Finally, the man dropped his cigarette and ground it into the earth with the toe of his shoe. He lifted his head quickly and peered into the darkness directly toward Harry. Just as abruptly, he turned away and followed the woman into the cottage.

Harry hadn't recognised the woman. From behind she looked like all of the mothers on the lake. But for one brief moment, as the man turned his head, the light from the window had fallen full on his face. The man was Harry's father.

****

Harry stood by the large birch where the night before a woman he didn't recognise had made love to his father. Made love sounds funny, Harry thought. Suggests romance. Courtship. Screwed was more like it. Fucked. Father of two fucks unknown woman.

He reached for the tree, now standing guiltless at the edge of the clearing, and tore off a strip of white bark.

It was still early and the cottage stood silent, its inhabitants just now becoming conscious of a new day. A wisp of smoke from the chimney indicated Harry's mother had lit the stove. She was most likely filling the coffee pot and placing it on the stove at that very moment. Then she would start breakfast.

Harry's family had guests. The Nashes, who lived in the cottage three doors down, had gone to the city for the weekend, and left their two sons and one daughter with Harry's family. The boys, twins between whom Harry could never differentiate, were three years older than Harry. The girl, Charlene, the same age.

Movement drew Harry's eyes to the bedroom window whose light the night before had exposed his father's infidelity. Inside, the youngest Nash stood before the mirror that hung above a set of drawers. She crossed her arms and raised her night shirt over her elbows and shoulders and tugged it free from the top of her head. Harry's eyes fell with her long, straight hair to the small, dark circles exposed on her chest. He moved behind the tree to watch.

Charlene stood still before the mirror. Her hands moved to her chest. She grasped each small mound and squeezed them together, creating a small valley. Dropped her hands, turned sideways, and pushed her chest forward. Stomach in! Chest out! Stand straight, soldier!

Harry watched Charlene and felt a stirring in his groin. He watched Charlene and thought of the strange woman with her legs wrapped around his father's waist. Thought of the force with which his father had assaulted the woman. For that is what it had looked like. An assault. A battering.

Harry watched Charlene and thought of the strange woman and of his own small penis inside her.

When Charlene turned from the mirror, pulled a bathing top over her head and disappeared, Harry walked quickly to the outhouse where he pulled out his penis and stroked himself, closing his eyes as the warmth from his groin spread.

A banging on the outhouse door jolted him.

"What the hell are you doing?" It was his father.

Harry spun and plunked himself onto the hole, forgetting to put the seat down and nearly plunging through to the crap-filled depths below.

Again his father shouted.

Harry struggled to his feet and quickly lowered the seat. "I'm going to the bathroom. You'll have to wait a minute."

Harry listened to his father's receding steps, then realised he did need to pee. He pushed, but despite the pressure in his bladder, nothing happened. He looked down at the slowly subsiding erection that dangled between his legs. He pushed harder, but still - nothing. Maybe he'd damaged something. What if he could never pee again? What if his bladder filled until it burst and he died? How would he explain that to his parents?

"Dear God," Harry whispered. "Just let me piss and I swear I'll never touch myself there again."

"You almost done?" His father had returned.

Harry fought the tears rising in his eyes and took a deep breath. "I'll be right out."

And he meant it. He was ready to run out of the outhouse. To confess all so his father could rush him to the hospital where doctors would slit open his stomach and drain his bladder. Or maybe there wasn't time. Maybe his father would simply lay him out on the kitchen table and give him a shot of scotch and a piece of wood to bite down on for the pain. Pour scotch across his belly to kill all germs and split him wide with the carving knife from the kitchen drawer.

Harry had seen it on tv. Operations in the wilderness. In westerns and war movies. Once even in a movie about a hunter who'd shot his friend, by accident, of course, and then had to save him or live with the guilt for the rest of his life.

But just when Harry thought all hope gone, just when he was readying himself to face his father, the first few drops trickled out. The drops became a small stream and then he was pissing at a heavenly rate. Harry breathed a loud sigh of relief. Almost laughed aloud.

"Jesus Christ," his father said. "You're such a weird kid."

****

"The competition is tough," Harry's mother said. "Tough and fierce. Now then. One more time. Receiving ..." She extended her hands forward, rolling her finger tips up from the palms of her hands until they extended toward the listener, as if prepared to receive a platter. " ... and receding ..." She rolled her hands over and back toward herself. Together, the gestures formed a motion similar to ocean waves massaging a beach.

Harry's older sister, Elizabeth, copied their mother's movements without enthusiasm.

"Elizabeth," their mother said. "That will never do. You have to work to keep a man's attention. They're not the brightest creatures, you know. Now, say it or you'll never get it right."

"Mother!"

"Trust me, Elizabeth. Tough and fierce."

Unnoticed at the corner of the cottage, Harry moved his hands in miniature imitation as Lizzie began to repeat their mother's words. Then he tired of his sister's lesson and approached the beach where Charlene lay on a towel. He leaned against a tree and watched her with new-found interest.

Harry's thoughts were interrupted by his father summoning him behind the cottage, where Harry found him with the twins. Each of the twins held a pellet rifle. His father held a thin, oblong box about three feet long, which he handed to Harry.

"Go ahead. Open it."

Harry placed the box on the ground, cut the tape using his father's knife, and removed the top.

"A rifle?"

"Of course it's a rifle," his father laughed. "A pellet gun. Go ahead. Take it out."

The twins gushed their approval.

"Damn right, she's a beaut," Harry's father said.

The metal cold and damp in Harry's hands, he lifted the rifle to his shoulder and peered along the barrel.

"Well. What do you think?"

Harry lowered the rifle. "It's great, I guess."

"What do you mean 'you guess.' Of course it's great. Come on. Got some pellets in my pocket. Let's try it out."

They practised shooting at tin cans until his father was satisfied Harry could operate his new rifle safely.

"Now. Let's get dinner."

"Yeah!" shouted the twins.

"You mean shoot something for real?"

"Of course that's what I mean. What good's a rifle if you don't use it?"

The twins again voiced their approval.

"Well, I'm not sure I want to kill anything."

"Of course you don't. No one does. But sometime you may have to. So now's the time to learn."

Once in the woods, Harry had a plan. He would miss everything, but would come close enough to satisfy his father. For a short time this worked, and although his father's words remained encouraging, and he continued to spot small birds and squirrels as Harry's quarry, only the twins succeeded and Harry could sense his father's growing frustration. But whether out of guilt for causing that frustration, or whether he simply missed, Harry was never sure. But his heart sank as his father and the twins cried out in unison, "You got him!" and Harry saw the tiny shape of a squirrel tumble from the gun's sights.

His heart pounding, Harry moved slowly to join the others at the base of a tree. At their feet lay a small, brown squirrel, its back legs splayed uselessly in either direction. With its front paws, the tiny creature was attempting to drag itself back to the safety of the tree. Harry gagged, unable to catch his breath, unable to turn away.

"Good shot, Hare. But now you have to finish him off."

Harry shook his head dumbly.

His father laid his hand on Harry's shoulder. "I know it's no fun, Harry, but you have to. Just put the end of the barrel to the back of his head and squeeze the trigger."

Harry did as he was told and missed. The twins chuckled.

"Don't use the sights. Just put the barrel right against it."

The pellet made a soft plop and the squirrel's body jumped, rolled to its side and scratched the air with its paws. Then it was still. Harry saw the small hole in the back of the animal's head. The small, red dot where the pellet had entered. Tears welled in his eyes.

His father was speaking, but Harry no longer heard. The rifle slipped from his hands and he turned and ran toward home. He heard his father yell, but didn't stop until he reached the side of the cottage where he crumpled against the wall.

When his father rounded the corner of the building, Harry tried to wipe away the evidence of his crying.

"Jesus Christ, Harry. It's only a squirrel. There's hundreds of them around." Then his father raised his hand holding the limp body of the squirrel by the tail. "Anyway, now I'm going to teach you how to skin it."

Harry protested, but he knew it would do no good. With tears streaming silently down his cheeks, and his father standing over him issuing instructions, Harry lay the blade of his father's knife to the belly of the dead animal.

****

During dinner his father related Harry's afternoon hunting experience, including his tears. The twins laughed.

"And still you made him do it?" Harry's mother said.

"Well, sure. He's got to learn sometime."

"What the hell is that supposed to mean? Since when is murdering squirrels something a boy has to learn?"

The children stopped eating and watched Harry's father.

He looked down at his plate, shrugged his shoulders. "You don't murder squirrels," he said. "You hunt them."

"And we know how you love easy targets," Harry's mother said. "You just have to kill everything good, don't you, you bastard!"

Harry never saw his mother raise the knife. He saw only a flash of silver and the knife bouncing off his father's forehead. Harry's mother leapt from her chair and bolted from the room.

Harry's father checked his forehead for blood and then looked at Harry. ""Christ," he said. "I sure hope you appreciate all the flak I take for you."

****

After dinner Lizzie and Charlene remained to clear the table while the boys fished off the dock for rock bass and crappies which they placed in a bucket. On the beach, Harry's father arranged wood for a bonfire.

As darkness fell, the fire was lit and all except Harry's mother approached. Before long one of the twins disappeared, then returned with three sticks which he sharpened at one end with his pocket knife. He handed one stick to his brother, another to Harry.

"Time to begin the ritual," he said.

"Oh, cripes," Charlene said. "Not again."

The twins stuck the pointed ends of their sticks into the fire and motioned for Harry to do the same. When the ends glowed hot, one twin extracted a fish from the bucket and lay it on the ground where it flopped with violent heaves of its head and tail. The twin pulled his stick from the fire and slowly pushed the glowing end against the side of the fish.

"Talk, Nazi pig"

The fish squirmed. The twin stabbed hard into its side. "Talk, Nazi pig, or die!"

The fish heaved to escape.

"This is sick," Elizabeth said.

Charlene wrinkled her nose in disgust. "They do it all the time."

The girls remained only long enough to see the stick approach the fish's eye.

By now the other twin was trying to shove his stick up the fish's gills. He looked at Harry. "Get your stick," he said.

Harry didn't move.

"This one's done," the first twin said, flipping the carcass into the fire. "Next!" he called to an imaginary waiter.

Harry did not join in the next ritual, nor the one after, but upon the twins' and his father's insistence, he began the fourth victim on his own. Tentatively, he pushed his stick against the side of the fish, felt his stomach turn as it had when he watched the squirrel tumble from its perch.

"Come on," he heard the twins tell him. "Make it talk. Yeah. Make it talk."

"It's only a crappie," his father said. "It can't feel anything."

Harry no longer heard his companions, no longer felt the knot in his stomach. He felt only the yielding of his victim's tiny body as he thrust his stick hard into its flesh. Heard only the sizzle of its watery eyeball melting under his hot touch.

He stabbed ferociously until the fish was a punctured canvass and both eyes were gone. Then he straightened and peered down at his handiwork for a moment before flipping the remains into the fire where he watched it smoulder and told himself it was only a crappie.

he thought it better

When Hedy gave him the news, Evan knew he could not show the relief he felt. He'd done the right thing and to act different now would diminish that. He'd done the right thing by forcing her to end their relationship. That way she'd be able to tell everyone it was her who called it quits. No matter how badly he'd behaved, she'd at least have that. Hell, he was being so good about it, it was a shame he couldn't tell her and have her see that he really wasn't so bad after all. That he really did have her best interests at heart.

"Arte asked me out."

"And ...?"

"I said yes."

That was a bit of a surprise. Arte was Evan's best friend in his class, although it was more by chance than by choice. There were only seven boys in Evan's class and the other were all short and not very funny except, of course, for Bruce and even then everyone knew there was something different about Bruce. He was always in love with the lead singer of some rock band. At fifteen in a small town with one school that ran from kindergarten through high school, being different was not a good thing.

Evan avoided the face that searched his own earnestly in hopes of some sign, some indication of what was going on inside his mind. Evan avoided the face and dug at the dirt that lay between them with the toe of his shoe and tried to look thoughtful and a little hurt. After a few more hums and haws they parted with the understanding that it was mostly his fault. He really was being damn good about the whole thing.

Evan did the same thing when Arte found him. "I hope you don't mind," Arte said. "You haven't been paying her much attention lately so I didn't think you'd mind."

"Nah," Evan said. "I guess we were just growing apart." He'd heard that in a movie only the night before and felt a twinge of pride at having thought to use it so quickly. "You guys will be great together."

Arte let out a deep breath Evan hadn't realized he was holding. "Thanks, Evan. You know you're my best friend." He said it as though it was a consolation prize. Evan would have preferred a hint of fear at the prospect of losing his friendship. "We can still do things together. I mean, not just you and me, but all three of us."

Evan shrugged. "Yeah," he said. "Sure we can. Just like always." Evan couldn't actually remember the three of them doing anything together, but it sounded good. But Arte was being a bit of a wanker suggesting it. As far as he knew, hadn't Hedy just dumped Evan? Where was the sympathy? Evan didn't like that Arte was thinking maybe he had something to do with it and was trying to make it up to him.

For the next few days Evan tried to avoid both Hedy and Arte. And for the most part Hedy let him be, although he did notice she seemed to be everywhere he went. But Arte was always coming up to him pretending like nothing had happened except Evan caught him a few times looking at him like he felt sorry for him or something. That pissed Evan off but good. After all, Evan had done what he'd done for Hedy's sake, not so Arte could walk around thinking he'd pulled one over on him and now wanted to somehow make it up to him.

Finally, Evan had enough and he caught up to Hedy as she was leaving the school grounds. "If you want," he said, "I'll walk you to your corner."

She smiled. "Why not?"

By the time they reached her corner, his plan was working perfectly and she invited him home to play billiards. In the basement they pushed the balls around a bit and then they were necking on the couch.

"I only went out with Arte to get back at you," Hedy said. "I knew it would drive you crazy, especially since you don't like him."

Evan nodded. "It did," he said. "What's in here." He reached inside her sweater and cupped her breast. Watched her eyes close and her mouth quiver as he did. It amazed him to have such an effect. Every time, it goddamned amazed him.

Then Hedy's mother called down to see if he was staying for dinner, and Hedy looked at him hopefully, but he shook his head. "I have to get home." He swung his feet to the floor and stood.

"Call me later."

The next day Hedy gave him a kiss at his locker. "How come you didn't call. I spoke to Arte."

"About what?"

"About us. What did you think?"

"Why did you do that?"

"I told him were going back out."

Evan kneeled to get books from the bottom of his locker. "We're not going back out, Hedy. What happened yesterday was just habit. It didn't mean anything." He looked up to see her staring blankly at him. "If we went back out, the same problems would be there. You were right when you said we had to break up. You're still right."

Hedy said nothing and he closed his locker. Said, "I have a class," and walked past her. He felt like a shit but he thought it was better everyone knew where they really stood. He felt like a shit but he liked it better than when he just felt relieved.

A Common Foe

We want a table where we can eat, drink and smoke our pot. Gregor says this in the bad Scottish accent Harry hates but that Gregor slips into whenever he's been drinking and feels cocky. He thinks it gives him a reason to be feisty and aggressive – in other words, to act like an asshole. Gregor has that chip on his shoulder a lot of short guys seem to have, always trying to prove that while they may be small, they're no pushover and good luck to the fellow who decides to test them. He also does the voice because somewhere back in the ages of the dinosaurs his family came over from Scotland and he wants people to know that for all the same reasons he has a chip on his shoulder.

The waiter gives Gregor a cockeyed smile which only encourages him. We can still smoke pot on the balcony, can't we? Gregor asks. Then he laughs and winks at Harry and practically nudges the poor waiter to show he's joking and tells the guy how when he lived here ten or twelve years ago you used to be able to smoke drugs in all the bars and restaurants. You would have still been in school, I imagine, laddie. It's the tourists who ruined this town, Gregor says, ignoring the fact that without the tourists there would be no town. Especially the bastards from Ontario, he adds.

The waiter gives him a sweet smile. I'm from Ontario, he says.

Gregor doesn't miss a beat. Aye, he says. But you live here now, don't you? You're from Whistler. How long have you been here?

A little over two years.

See. That's exactly what I mean. You're a local. It's the bloody tourists I'm talking about.

The waiter can see there's not much point in continuing this conversation and steers them to a table on the balcony while Gregor reiterates how long ago he lived here. I bet you were still in school, he repeats.

There's two women sitting at the next table and even though Gregor and Harry are with Shirl and Mona, Gregor gives them the eye when they look up as he takes his seat. To their credit, they turn away without so much as nod. Gregor could have been a blank wall for all the interest they show, which prompts another of his standard lines. "Bloody dykes," he says. Then he turns to Shirl and makes a big show of how happy he is to be with her, which is a load of shit coming from him because usually he treats her like a little brother that he's got to drag around because his parents are out of town. Most of the time she takes it but not without giving some right back at him if she has the energy which she doesn't seem to right now. She just shakes his arm from her shoulder and pushes away the face he extends toward her with exaggerated pursed lips meant for a big showy display kiss and goes back to talking to Mona, whom she's known forever, which is why they're all up here together in the first place.

Gregor simply laughs and tells Harry she'll get hers later. Harry looks at Shirl and decides there probably won't be too much later. She's got that fed up look that says she'll stick around until something better comes along, but if that doesn't happen soon, she'll leave anyway. Harry doesn't think there's anything wrong with that, a woman over thirty on her own. He thinks there's something admirable about it, something attractive about the ability to stave off convention by not marrying the first asshole who proclaims his love for her. A sexy kind of power. For the life of him, Harry can't understand why women feel more pressure than men to get married in the first place. It's clearly the men who get the better end of that stick.

****

Gregor is feeling good. He hasn't looked back at the two women at the next table since he sat down and he feels good about snubbing them. The unsociable snots. It wasn't like he was trying to pick them up. He hadn't even said a word, had simply smiled.

But now he feels good and he looks out over the courtyard before turning back to his friends. It is a melancholy night, he announces, feeling good with himself for showing some sensitivity to their surroundings. And no better place to be with good friends. He raises his glass in toast and their glasses clink and everyone takes a swig and sits back for an awkward moment.

That's a funny word to use, Harry says. Melancholy.

What are you talking about? Look around you, man. It's kind of like this sad, pensive moment.

I suppose.

The slap on his arm takes Harry by surprise. He jerks around to find Gregor's face in his, the angry spittle bouncing off his lips as he speaks. You've got a problem. You've got a problem with any word you didn't use first. Big master's in English and now no one else knows how to talk. Gregor has raised his hand and is shaking his finger in Harry's face as he speaks.

Harry looks beyond the finger at the strained anger in Gregor's clenched face and thinks: This moron does not deserve Shirl, and she can certainly do better than him. This is what runs through Harry's mind. His mouth says, Hey man. I just said it was funny word to use. I really don't give a shit.

Gregor! This comes from Shirl. Gregor lowers his finger and settles back into his chair. For a guy who doesn't give a shit, he tells Harry, you've always got a lot to say.

Harry holds out his cigarette pack like a general peace offering.

Holds the match scooped in the palm of his hand and smiles at the girls as he gives them a light. Mona does not smile back which doesn't surprise Harry and he avoids her eyes. Shirl gives him a quick smile, but Harry decides it is resigned instead of curt. And maybe a bit apologetic, which convinces him she really doesn't deserve such an asshole.

Recent movies bring up the topic of war. I can't believe what that prick Baden Powell did to the Canadians at Normandy, Harry says. All because he wanted that invasion under his belt. Cement his place in glorious history as a great leader. What an asshole. But what did the Brits care? Those were only Canadian troops they were sending in.

You talking about Dieppe? Gregor asks.

I guess so, Harry says.

Well if you're talking about Dieppe, my friend, then you should get your goddamned facts straight. It was Dieppe, not Normandy, where the Canadians got slaughtered. And it was Lord Mountbatten who sent them in, not Baden Powell. Lord Baden Powell was the founder of the boy scouts. You should know that for Christ's sake. You must have been a goddamn cub scout. There's no way you weren't.

Harry says he knows who Baden Powell was. He just thought that was who'd been in charge. So what?

So what? Gregor looks at him with disgust. If you're going to tell a story, at least get your goddamned facts straight. That's what's so what. My uncle was in the Second World War, so don't try and tell me any stories about it if you don't know what the hell you're talking about.

****

Gregor hasn't worked in three years. He says it's because of his back. Injured in a car accident and can barely make it off the tennis court if he plays for more than an hour at a time. Otherwise, he's a fisherman, which in today's world means you're unemployed and angry. Put that together with the aforementioned short-man syndrome and you've got one volatile little bastard. When he gets together with his three brothers it's like being inside a molecule with atoms bashing each other around. Talk about your negative energy. Two of them is enough to clear any room of intelligent discussion. Bullshit and brawn before brains. The ability to batter any opposing view into submission.

Harry figures that, if it came down to it, he could take Gregor in a fair fight, but how do you justify a bottle in the face? I'm going for a piss, he says.

Shirl is there when he comes out of the bathroom. I'm sorry about him, she says. Don't be. It's not your fault.

I know, she says. I don't even know why I'm with him. And then she gives Harry the same resigned smile as before and he tells her it's okay and gives her a peck on the cheek and before he knows it they're swapping spit right there in the hallway where anyone could catch them. Then Shirl pulls away and says, my god, what are we doing? And Harry sort of shrugs and shakes his head in way that he thinks will look confused, as though he shares her concern which, naturally, he cannot.

****

When Harry returns to the table, Gregor asks him if he took a book with him to the can. For Christ sakes, you been gone forever. Just about to send out a search party, weren't we? Gregor winks at Mona as though she's enjoying his little digs at Harry, and she sort of half smiles back out of duty and then she gives Harry one of those looks that says I told you not to say anything - the kind of look you give a kid who's just done something you asked him not to, but it's not a bad enough thing to really get in trouble for, at least not right there and then if you're in public. It's a cross between anger and disappointment. It would be more effective if it showed only disappointment but Mona doesn't have any kids so she hasn't had the practice necessary to remove the anger. Only real mothers can do that.

Gregor watches Harry take his seat. He doesn't like this guy, with his masters and his travelling and his black clothes. Always black. Like a mortician hit hard by the recession who's never fully recovered. Everything just a bit tattered. Just a bit ill-fitting. Gregor knows Harry does it on purpose. Part of his I'm-a-fucking-writer costume. Goddamned phoney, that's what he is. Writer, my ass. A couple of short stories that wouldn't hold the imagination of a toadstool. Why doesn't he just admit it? He's no better than me. Christ, I'll start calling myself a goddamn consultant. Isn't that what every unemployed bastard with an inkling of pride does? Never unemployed. No bloody way, my friend, that that was me you saw standing in the UI line. Make that EI; isn't that's what they call it now. Employment insurance. Like a change in name is going to make a big difference to the poor bastard who's stuck standing in the goddamn line so some pencil-pushing pin head can look down at him and review his form like he's an illiterate sap who can't even be trusted to fill out his name and address without screwing it up.

When Shirl returns, Gregor again watches Harry. He's not sure what, but there's something going on between them. Noticed it that afternoon. The two of them looking at each other like they were appraising used cars. Nothing overt. Just interest. Well, screw them. Screw them both. If that's what Shirl wants, then more power to her. If she wants some pompous, mouthy, bastard faggot who knows shit about the war but still goes on about it in that irritating authoritative voice of his, like everyone is hanging on to every one of his boring words, like he's the only one who knows anything, then who is Gregor to stand in her way? Fuck her. She's beginning to bore him anyway. Always cackling on about something, like he's going to change at this point in his life. What for? He has friends. People who like him, who understand him and his sense of humour which, he's the first to admit, isn't necessarily for everyone. But damn he has his moments.

And some people appreciate it. Like Joey Donnell. Now there's a regular guy who appreciates a good joke. Doesn't need to be some clever insight into the human condition. Damn it, Joey lives the human condition. He used to be an electrician for Christ's sake. He knows the value of manual labour, of working with your hands. Without guys like him, how would that smart-ass Harry write? No power, no computer to sit in front of waiting for his divine muse to come, the phoney bastard.

No. His humour may not be for everyone, but damn, Gregor has his moments.

Shit, he doesn't want to be here in the first place. If it wasn't for Shirl's and Mona's friendship, he wouldn't be. Shirl's and Mona's friendship. Now that adds an interesting twist to what Gregor thinks is going on. How will that go over? Your best friend steals your boyfriend. Not well, he hopes.

****

Harry feels the aggression mounting in Gregor and wants to normalise things so they can at least make it through dinner without a chair being cracked over someone's skull. He's thinking of the list of topics not allowed for discussion that Mona gave him before they came. Fishing is right up on top. Everyone's pissed off with the goddamned government who can't seem to avoid messing up everything they touch. And work. Never talk about work around the chronically unemployed. Like that was a big problem for Harry. Oh, do let me tell you about the story I'm writing. Like most of the moronic masses, in which he includes Gregor, can understand let alone appreciate a goddamned thing he writes. All they want is plot. A beginning, a middle, an end. Everything wrapped up in the time it takes to have a good shit so they don't have to wait until their next bowel movement to finish the thing. And please, don't, whatever the hell you do, make them think. Give them their opinion on a platter a six-year-old can understand.

While he's thinking of a topic suitable to the idiosyncrasies of the moron seated beside him, Harry is conscious of Mona watching him. They've been going out a few months and she knows him pretty well – or so she keeps telling him - so she probably knows something's up by the way he slunk back to his seat and then tried to be all up and interested after he sat down, not to mention how he's avoiding looking at Shirl for more than a few seconds at a time, and then only when he's talking – so as to include her – or when she is, so as to display just the right amount of polite interest without going overboard into the fascination zone. Harry has to be careful about this. He knows he has a bad habit of agreeing a bit too heartily with a woman's opinion if he's interested in her, and Mona knows it too. She doesn't mind when he's a bit flirtatious at parties or in bars, but flirting with her best friend at the dinner table would be pushing it. Harry knows that from experience. All in all, Harry's feeling pretty pleased with himself for keeping things on an even keel.

****

Harry's doing it again. Mona hates it when he gets that smug look on his face. Like he's got something going on that no one else knows about. Christ, why doesn't he just whip it out of his pants and lay it on Shirl's plate and get it over with. At least then maybe they could try to have a nice time.

God, why was it so hard to find people you can just do stuff with and not have to always worry about what you say or how you say it or who you say it to? She never had to worry about this shit before, not when she lived in Toronto. There at least, she knew where she stood with people. Or most people.

She still can't believe that Jackie came on to Harry when they went back to visit last month, although she should have expected it. That's Jackie's style. And Harry's such a conceited jerk at times, he really believed it was about him. Even after Mona tried to explain it had nothing to do with him, that it wouldn't have mattered if he'd been a total moron Jackie would have still sought him out because that's what she does. Steals boyfriends. Not that she needs them. Jackie is blond, good looking, and smart. Her parents must have really messed her up somewhere along the line for her to still be so insecure. For God's sakes, Mona wants to tell her. Get over it!

But this is different. The stuff going on between Harry and Shirl is far too subdued, nothing like the overt flirtations Harry is normally involved in. Basically, he knows only one way to relate to women, as potential sex partners. That's what once he told her. That every woman is a potential fuck. This was before they started seeing each other, when they were doing the sexual sparring thing at some bar Mona hates. A university hangout with old wooden chairs and tables that don't match and the perpetual smell of stale beer and cigarettes. Harry loves the place but now only goes there with his friends from school days. Mona went with him a couple of times, but stopped once she realised that stepping through the door makes Harry a complete jerk. He starts acting as though he's still a graduate student and that the students who belong there are actually interested in what this old fart has to say. Self-delusion is a curious and powerful force.

Now Gregor is a whole other study in that area. A self-proclaimed expert on the issues of fishing, teaching, government policy, immigration, and anything else that happens to land on the conversation table. Don't even get Mona started on Gregor. She can't help thinking of the first night they met. Gregor stinking drunk banging his fist on the end of the dinner table and telling them all to shut the hell up with their stupid ideas because real life was happening all around them. Like he knows a lot about real life, holed up in his apartment bitching about the Americans fishing while he sits on his ass counting his haemorrhoids waiting for the government to tell him his boat can go out. It's not even his boat for Christ's sake. He only works on it.

For the life of her, Mona cannot figure out what Shirl is doing with him. She deserves someone more like, well, like Harry. She's not the most talkative person, which goes perfectly with someone like Harry who never shuts up and who doesn't really give a shit about anyone else's opinion unless it supports his own. On the one hand, Mona likes this about him, that he has an opinion on almost anything. On the other, it drives her crazy because knowing nothing about a subject doesn't stop him from believing he's right.

If Mona is to really think about it, she would have to admit she has never taken their relationship seriously. They have fun together, especially when there's no one else involved, but in a crowd his confidence, which borders on conceit, can be such a pain in the ass. So if, or rather, when their relationship ends, it won't be the end of the world. It can't go on forever; there's no way they'll ever end up married or even living together. But how would she feel if he started seeing Shirl? Or even worse, if he left Mona for Shirl. Mona knows why it might happen. Shirl is in trouble and to Harry there is no greater aphrodisiac. He loves to play the part of the great white knight. But it just would be too much, not because Mona would care, but think of the public humiliation. Everyone would think Shirl had stolen him away. That would not reflect well upon Mona. She hates it, but she always worries about how things will look.

Mona will have to have that awkward little talk with Harry on Monday. She isn't worried about breaking his heart. She knows the only reason he'll be in any way hurt is because she did it first. Things like that matter to him.

****

Gregor is bored. Dinner is over and all this talk about books and movies is about as much fun as conversing with tree stumps. A bloody bore. He tried to talk about the fishing crisis, but no one was into that. They couldn't possibly understand anyway, little yuppie office-bound scum. I need a drink, he says. He shouts across the balcony to the waiter who's standing at another table, and who, as far as Gregor's concerned, is being an ignorant ass and ignoring them. Hey laddie. Four Courvoisier. He holds up four fingers.

The waiter nods and continues talking to the other table.

That guy is the worst goddamn waiter, Gregor says. And I don't think he likes us, the little Ontario dickhead.

No kidding, agrees Harry. He's goddamn useless.

Gregor shouts at the guy again and this time he comes over. Can I get you something? he asks, all sweet and nice like Gregor's his best friend and it's his big pleasure to serve him. Bloody irritating is what he is. No, Gregor says. We're sitting here letting the crap you served us digest before it regurgitates and we have to suffer through it again.

The waiter's clearly taken back but he's dealt with this shit before. Gorbies, he thinks. Pathetic tourists. Everyone thinks they're a local and deserve special treatment if they've even set foot in the place before. Was there something wrong with the food? he asks.

Gregor will not look up. Nah, he says. Just bring us four Courvoisier.

Yeah, says Harry. Four Courvoisier.

The waiter smiles. Maybe, he says, you've had enough to drink. Shall I bring you all coffee instead?

This time Gregor looks up. If I wanted a goddamn coffee, that's what I would have asked for. And as near as I can remember, I didn't say anything about coffee. Did anyone hear me mention coffee?

The girls are clearly not impressed with the turn of events and remain quiet, but Harry sees the opportunity to stand behind Gregor, to forget their differences and to unite against a common foe. I, he says, did not hear a thing about coffee. But perhaps you're right about the Courvoisier, he tells the waiter. Make mine a Grand Marnier.

Whatever, says Gregor. Just bring the drinks, lad, and don't try to be telling us what we want and don't want. What a dickhead, Gregor says after the waiter leaves.

Damn right, Harry says. Got that snotty little superiority

complex prevalent in his field. Like being a waiter actually takes more than two brain cells. And he's not even in Vancouver where at least he can claim to be an actor for the appearance of ambition and respectability.

Gregor elects to say nothing about writers, just nods in agreement as Harry continues.

Now that's painful. All those idiot waiters wasting their time fighting for parts in the pieces of shit that pass for theatre these days. If I hear of one more goddamn musical, I'll have to shoot someone. They made Kiss of the Spider Woman into a one, for Christ's sake. What's next? Kosovo, The Musical?

When the waiter returns Gregor asks what he'll do for a real job, later, when the resort thing grows old. The waiter simply smiles. Hadn't even thought about it, he says. Can I get you anything else?

Harry can tell the waiter is just blowing them off and doesn't really blame him. He's worked the bar scene before and there's nothing worse than the misplaced superiority of the loser drunk. They sidle up to the bar and immediately start confiding in you about the assholes in the place as though only you and they know what's really what. And they only include you because they know you're not there by choice and that if you didn't have to work this shift you wouldn't be caught anywhere near this place and these losers who surround you. That and because you have control of the bar.

Harry tells the waiter to bring the bill and then they try to figure out the tip and Gregor is going on about how bad the service was and what an asshole the waiter is and how there's no goddamn way he's going to leave fifteen percent. Ten bucks is enough for anybody to serve a meal, he says, ignoring the fact that his and Shirl's portion of the bill comes to well over one hundred dollars. Harry tries to move him up a bit, partially because the service wasn't really that bad and partially because he was in the business and can't stand to leave less than fifteen percent on principle, but Gregor's not budging. He tells Harry to leave whatever he wants, but he's leaving ten bucks and that's it.

So Harry writes ten dollars on the gratuities line of his credit card receipt, but as they leave, Gregor sees him hand the waiter an extra ten and say something about being sorry they hassled him and now Gregor is really pissed. That little snot-nosed Harry. Goes along with just about everything on the surface, but scratch a little deeper and he's always doing things that make him look better than everyone else. And for what? The only ones who will know are people like the waiter, people they don't even know and will likely never see again. Like they could ever do anything to help Harry.

Yeah, Gregor's pissed off at the little bleeding-heart snob, but he'll wait until they get to the car before he says anything. He doesn't want the waiter to see them fighting.

All the Useless Things

The alleyway leads north, away from the street where blue jeans drape over tables littered with cigarettes, imitation Barbie Dolls and plastic machine guns. Away from vendors slouched against brick walls, mouths hanging loose and wet in sleep. Away from windows shuttered tight against the dust and soot that rise from the street like a permanent fog.

It advances where shadows slope behind a wall built thick against conspirators. Where garbage cans stationed like drunken soldiers, caps skewed crazily atop overflowing rotted vegetable matter, amuse dredging rats.

Passes beneath towering metal cranes, silhouettes black against the morning sky, elongated beaks poised to tear at buildings and leave heaps of regurgitated brick and plaster behind.

It curls beneath fish gutted and split wide. Beneath pucker-skinned fowl and air-blackened slabs of anonymous meat lynched beside laundry on rusty wires running slack from window frame to window frame.

Winds past a woman in miniskirt, with thick, brown, stockings bunched about her ankles. Leaning against a doorway smoking a cigarette, watching without interest the entrance to the brick shithouse twenty yards distant where the alleyway ends. Where the man has gone to relieve himself, his semen still warm and sticky between her thighs.

In the shithouse the man pisses into a black tub too long

neglected, tugs at his pants, changes his mind and hunkers low, slinging his naked buttocks across a jagged hole smashed into the concrete floor. Searches the shadows for newspaper to wipe his ass.

Behind the woman, a small child cries out. She cocks her head, chooses to ignore and wraps her tired lips around the cigarette, inhales deep and discards the butt beside the cylinders of coal and sawdust too damp to burn, bought from a crooked merchant with rotted rat-teeth and now piled high and useless against the once red brick wall.

The child steps into the doorway beside the woman, tugs on her skirt and receives a slap. Moves away, rubbing his eyes, and squats beside the smouldering butt, his piss squirting through the slit in the crotch of his pants, splattering his black, road-toughened feet. He pushes on the crippled remains of a bamboo cart to right himself, then watches the man emerge from the shitter.

The man pauses and begins a grumbling deep in his throat, works the flem slowly to the back of his tongue. Sends a thick glob sailing. Pulls a cigarette from his shirt pocket and lights it. As he approaches, he kicks at a bottle missed by the shrunken relic who scours the alleyways for the two *jiao* return per bottle. Kicks it smashing against the shattered and decaying bones of a prehistoric bicycle where it tinkles like a distorted wind chime. Pushes the woman in through the doorway ahead of him.

The boy peers through the crack between the double wooden doors. Wonders at the whiteness of the man's skin. Watches the white buttocks rise and fall above his mother.

Afterward, the man stands in the doorway and smokes. Looks at the boy and smiles.

Ni shi meiguoren ma? the boy asks.

Bu shi. Not American. Not anything.

****

You think you can fuck our women whenever you please?

The question takes Robin by surprise. Most taxi drivers want to sell him women. He pretends not to understand.

Fucking *laowei*. Fucking rich *meiguo* bastard. The driver smiles as he speaks. Watches Robin in his rear-view mirror.

In the reflection, Robin sees the driver's tobacco-stained, intermittent teeth. He turns away and looks out the window.

The driver continues to watch him. Your fucking girlfriend is in for it now, he says. I know where she lives, and soon the police will too.

At his hotel, Robin throws ten *yuan* on the passenger seat without looking. Hears the driver insult his mother's vagina. The doormen smile as they hold the doors open for him.

****

In his suite Robin stops and listens. He listens for running water, for music. For the sound of papers being shuffled.

Instead he finds one of her gloves beneath a sofa cushion. A barely used tube of lipstick in the washroom cabinet. Dark red. A colour she hated - he liked. He leaves these things where he finds them. As though she's just lost them. Sometimes Robin thinks she left them on purpose. Tell-tale ghosts of past demands and transgressions. She's been gone almost six months.

Robin thinks of going to work. Phones his office and tells them he's sick. They try to sound understanding. Say they hope he's feeling better by tomorrow. But both he and they are bored with this game.

He pulls a bottle of scotch from the freezer. Considers the time - too early to start drinking. Retrieves a glass from the bathroom and doesn't bother with ice.

****

She's been gone since the dinner party. At first only a couple of blocks. Now across the Pacific.

Robin hadn't meant for it to go that far. For her to go that far. But he never knows when to stop, when to be quiet. Never knows where to draw the line.

"Helen has a new friend," Robin had told their dinner guests. "Isn't that right, Helen?"

She'd returned his smile with undisguised sarcasm and said nothing.

"Yes. A new friend. A boyfriend actually. Meets him for lunch - what - about once a week? Would that be correct, Dear? Unless there are times I don't know about. Are there times I don't know about, Helen?"

Helen didn't think their guests wanted to hear about it.

"Why is that, Helen? Why wouldn't they want to hear about your new friend? We're just talking about what we all do. How we keep ourselves amused in this god-forsaken city. I'm just telling them one of the things that you do." He turned and waved his glass toward their friends. "This is interesting, isn't it? You do want to know what Helen does, don't you?"

Silence.

"There. You see. They are interested in what you do. I think you should tell us all about your new friend. Why don't you start with his name? He's not just anyone, is he? He's Chinese. A local. What's his name, Helen?"

"Li Peng."

"Li Peng. The prime minister. Oh that's very good, Helen. One of the things I've always loved about you. Your sense of humour."

Robin filled his own wine glass, then everyone else's, and lighted a cigarette.

At the far end of the table one of their guests, Andrew, cleared his throat. “Very nice wine, Robin.”

Robin continued, appearing not to hear. "I can certainly imagine why he'd want your friendship, you being a *laowei* and all. These Chinese do like to practice their English. How did you meet him, Dear? You never told me how you met. Did he approach you on the street and ask if you'd like to be his friend? Walk up and ask where you're from?"

Helen did her best to ignore him. "The wine's South African."

"That's how it happens, you know.” Robin looked around the table. “But why am I telling you? You've lived here as long as us. The way they just come up on the street and ask for your telephone number.

"'Hello. Where are you from? Oh, Canada. Canada very nice country.' You could tell them you were from fucking Siberia and they'd still say 'Oh, Siberia. Siberia very nice country.’

Robin addressed the woman beside him. “You, Lorna, with your blond hair, must get this all the time. Then the telephone calls start. Would you like to have lunch? Would you like to take me to a western restaurant? Would you like to come and meet my family? Would you like to fucking sponsor me to go to university in Canada?

“Has he asked you that yet, Helen? Has he asked you about helping him get to Canada?”

Helen glared. Robin drank and lighted another cigarette with the one he’d just smoked.

He ground the spent butt in the ashtray. "That is what they all want, isn’t it? To get out of this fucking place.”

“Christ,” Andrew said. “Wouldn't you? You can't get anything here."

“This place is far more interesting than anything home has to offer,” Helen said. “You both sound like you’ve been here too long.”

"We're not talking about being a goddamn tourist, Helen. I, for one, would definitely want out. I think anyone in their right mind would. Unless, of course, you're a member of the government. Perhaps your friend is, Helen. Or a PSB spy? Public Security likes to know they've got all the bases covered. Make sure there's no secret housewives' association planning to undermine the government. Planning to poison the minds of the Chinese public. Planting the seeds of discontent with malicious lies about democracy and freedom with their *aiyees*. Imagine hundreds of cleaning ladies marching the streets protesting, mops held high in defiance."

"Don't even start with *aiyees*," Lorna said. "They're simply impossible. Did we tell you? We had to fire our *aiyee* last week. It turned out she was stealing my clothes. Do you know how we found out? She came to work wearing one of my shirts!"

"I told her she should have asked for it back," Andrew said.

"I couldn't wear it after that. It would have been filthy. They wash their clothes in the canals, you know."

"It would have taught her a lesson, though. Can you imagine? Running home through the streets in only her bra." Lorna and Andrew chuckled lightly. Waited to see what effect their diversion would have.

"Or perhaps it's me he's interested in," Robin said. "Does he ask many questions about me, Helen? About what your husband does? Why his company is really here. Does he ask about me, Helen?"

"Oh, please!"

"No. I would expect not. That would be too obvious. Not to mention insulting. You don't go to lunch with a married woman seeking attention and spend the time asking about her husband. No. I'm sure your friend is nothing like that. I'm sure yours is only interested in you for your witty conversation.

"I assume that is why you have this new friend whose name

you won't tell us. Seeking the attention I fail to provide because I'm working my ass off. I must admit, there's some validity to that argument."

Robin turned to Lorna and Andrew. "You must understand that. You both have jobs that keep you at the office until late every evening. Imagine what it would be like if you didn't have a job. If you didn't work. If all you had to do each day was go to the gym, meet friends for coffee. Christ, even the shopping is done for you.

"And I admit, I'm not perfect. Maybe I could make it home a little earlier if I wanted. Leave some work for the next morning. Not everything is so life threatening that it can't wait.

"But that's not what I'm paid for. Not why any of us are here. They pay us to do our jobs well and fast. Why else would they pay for our housing? Give us drivers. Not to mention our salaries.

"But maybe that doesn't matter to Helen. Maybe she chooses to conveniently forget about that. About where we'd be if it wasn't for my job. If it wasn't for my long hours. Is that right, Helen? Is it easier just not to think about that?

"Of course, then she'll probably say something about the nights I'm out late that have nothing to do with work. The nights I'm at Minders, or Frank's. But then, as you know, she's usually with me. But maybe you choose to forget that, too. Is that what you do, Helen?

"And yes, sometimes I have the tendency to stay out a little bit late. Who doesn't. If you're having fun what the hell does the time matter? Especially with the long goddamn hours I put in at work. I deserve a little time to play. But I don't have to tell you two about that. You know."

"We all certainly tend to drink a bit more here than normal," Andrew said. "Have to. Necessity. So bloody stressful. Can't even ..."

"I guess Helen feels that's reason enough to seek male companionship elsewhere. Not that I think anything's going on. I know they're just friends. But you both know how important face is in this country. Can you imagine what that would do to my reputation at the office if anyone was to find out my wife meets with another man? A Chinese man. Can you imagine what they'd think of me? The loss of face I would incur.

"But I guess that doesn't really concern you, does it, Helen? You're a poor neglected housewife seeking a little attention. A small token of appreciation from a member of the opposite sex. Anyone of the gender will do. As long as he's got a penis hanging between his legs and makes you feel desirable. Makes you feel special. I guess that's all that matters.

Shut up, Robin thinks. Why couldn't I have just shut up?

Helen turned toward Robin and smiled. "There is no Chinese man," she said.

Why do I never know when to draw the line?

"There's only Peter Denton."

That was not supposed to happen.

"The Australian."

Some things cannot be taken back.

"And of course I fuck him."

****

Robin awakens and wretches into the toilet. He drinks a beer standing under a cold shower, dresses and leaves the hotel to walk to Maggie's.

Robin is sick. He's sick of the marauding procession of rusty, faded-blue trucks and dull, yellow taxis that blast their horns as they throw coal-black exhaust into his face. Sick of dodging lengthy, ancient buses with disintegrating accordion mid-sections that block his route, of conductors and drivers screeching price and destination over scoring speakers in a never-ending sales pitch to prospective riders.

And he is sick of the beggars on the sidewalk displaying stunted and distorted limbs beside murky vendors who scatter across his path like mice, their stash of CD's illegal and hunted by plainclothes police in semi-pursuit.

He cuts off Xinyuan South Road, walks down to the canal where fishermen have nets sunk low in the river, corners pinned down by long spider-leg poles. Robin pauses to watch as one fisherman drags the bottom clear where his net will lie. Swings a grapple in a slow and steady arc. Releases it to sail out into the water, landing with a small splash. Leaves the line loose while the grapple sinks, then hauls it in slow and steady as if he's already hooked a fat round carp. Pulls the plastic bags from the hooks and then begins to swing it again.

The fisherman is old, rust-skin the colour of the grapple. Wears a Mao suit, a Mao hat. Now not so common in Beijing. He turns toward Robin as he hauls in his last throw. Doesn't smile at first. Then displays sporadic, nicotine-teeth, and Robin is surprised to find the old man's smile is in response to his own. He raises his hand in a half-greeting, but the old man has turned away to finish his task.

At the east third ring road Robin turns north, back up toward Maggie's. Passes vendors of fruits and toilet paper, vegetables and posters, competing for the same coins hidden in passer-by's pockets. Passes shoe repair men sitting side-by-side on stunted stools like aged gargoyles, one hunched over his tiny, hand-powered sewing machine while a woman balances impatiently on one foot. Sidewalk urchins scramble about Robin's feet like beach crabs on the bloated body of a seal washed ashore. Repeat the one English word they've been taught. Money.

Normally he ignores them. Pushes them away with his squash racquet. Or his briefcase. Doesn't want the filth from their hands to mark his clothing. Today he places a few coins in their hands.

Watches them scurry back to their beggar master where he sits drinking beer and smoking with his friends beneath the staircase leading up to a large western-style department store.

Robin ducks into the darkness and solitude that is Maggie's. Plops onto a bar stool and orders a Corona.

A woman slides onto the stool beside him. She is short and heavy. Imported from the north. Mongolian.

She flashes a piano key-board smile and asks his name. "I like know you better, Rawin," she says.

It would be nice to believe that, Robin thinks. Just once, it would be nice to believe that.

Then he calls to the bartender and orders them each another beer.

Worm Man

The last day I saw him, he was dangling a worm above his upturned face. It squirmed between his fingers and mud fell into his open mouth. He lowered it slowly and then raised it, keeping his eyes on us the entire time. On our shocked and disgusted faces. We knew he probably wouldn't put it in, but there was always the chance he would. He lowered and raised the worm like that until we squirmed with revolted anticipation and then - pop - it was in his mouth in a motion so quick we never saw where it actually went. But the worm would be gone and he'd be chewing and making yummy noises like it tasted really good. And we'd never be sure if he ate it or not. He was, after all, retarded. Or at least we thought he was. No one knew for certain. But he couldn't talk and that was enough for us to assume he wasn't normal. Wasn't right in the head.

He showed up periodically in the field behind our school. Came down out of the woods behind where he dug for worms. Came down during recess when the kids were out playing. Or during lunch break.

He came down wearing the only set of clothes I can remember seeing him in. His coat was the kind my father wore. My father called it a raincoat, but that wasn't what I would have called it. It wasn't rubberised, or yellow, or anything I'd ever associated with raincoats. It was more of an overcoat. The kind tall riders wore in the westerns we saw at the only English cinema in town.

Randolph Scott was my favourite cowboy. He wasn't

particularly dashing or anything, but he had a cool way about him. You never saw him get upset or angry about anything. If there was a problem, and there always was, he just strapped on his six-shooter, climbed on his horse and took care of it.

My dad climbed into his Mercury everyday and went to his office. Sometimes he took us with him and dropped us off at school. I liked going with him better than taking the bus, but I would've preferred to go by horse.

The school had different entrances for girls and boys - it was marked right over the doorways – but the field was for everyone. Once you were off the field, though, you weren't even allowed on the wrong side of the school. There was a girl in my class who wrote that she loved me in large chalk letters on her side of the school. I love Henry Lonsdale. Everyone knew who wrote it. She used to call out to me whenever she saw me outside of school. Even when I was with my friends. It got so bad I had to speak to her about it. That's what my mom always said when one of us was in trouble. I'll have to speak to your father about this.

So I spoke to Sally, that's the girl, about it. I tried to do it where no one would see. Tried to be kind about it. I told her I didn't want her talking to me anymore or writing anything else about me. I told her I didn't like her, not even as a friend, and that she just better cut it all out. Then I turned and ran away. But not before my friends had seen us. They started teasing me so I had to tell them I hated her.

The truth of it was, I didn't hate her. I even sort of liked her. But she'd made things too difficult, so I guess it wasn't really my fault - the way things turned out, I mean.

I know Randolph would have dealt with things differently, but he had a horse.

So Worm Man - that's what we called him, Worm Man, like a mock super hero – would come down onto the field and start pretending to eat worms and a group of us would crowd around to watch. We didn't crowd too close though, because none of us wanted to actually touch him. His coat was like my dad's, but not really. It looked like one my dad would have thrown away about a million years ago. It was hard to even tell what colour it was it was so old and dirty. And all the edges, not just the bottom ones, were torn and jagged like an old rag. And the same thing went for his pants.

In general, his clothes looked like him. Grey. He was one big grey mess. Never clean shaven, but he didn't have a beard either. He just sort of had patches of hair that grew anywhere they pleased and never got any shorter or longer. Even on the top of his head. And in between the hair were patches of splotched grey skin. Like the colour of the ashes after a fire's had water poured over it – some places black, some places grey.

Worm Man could never hang around the yard for long. As soon as teachers saw him, they waved him away with the back of their hands like they were shooing away a fly. They didn't push him or anything like that. You could see they didn't want to hurt him. Some you almost thought felt sorry for him, but they didn't like him hanging around. They said school was private property reserved for our use only. I didn't think his being there was that big a deal. It was a pretty big field.

So Worm Man was dangling the worm above his mouth like always, and the mud was dropping like it always did, when Donnie Smith pushed Denise Aubain into him on a dare from Darren Latramouile. And that's when the Worm Man let go the worm.

We watched the worm fall. Like slow motion in a movie. We'd been watching it carefully to try and catch the exact moment it disappeared, to see where it actually went. Well, it disappeared all right. Right down the front of Denise's dress. For a few seconds it felt like nothing was going to happen. Everyone frozen with shock, half waiting to see what Denise was going to do. And then Denise was screaming bloody blue murder and thrashing around on the ground and the only one to move was Worm Man.

He fell to his knees beside Denise and tried to grab her shoulders to stop her from thrashing and then I saw one of his hands go down her top.

I knew he only wanted the worm. Knew he was only trying to help the best he could. But Denise was crying and the front of her dress was ripped and Worm Man was being held by two male teachers until the police could get there and we were being herded back to class like cows on a cattle drive. Every time I tried to turn around to see what was happening a hand pushed my shoulder to make me face straight ahead again. Off to the side I could see Miss Rabbit, my teacher last year in grade four, hugging Denise as she gently moved her toward the school until Mr. Givens, the vice principal, hurried toward them and gathered Denise in his arms and half ran with her to the back entrance of the school where only teachers were allowed to go in. And as they were about to enter I caught a glimpse of Denise's face and I could see she was still crying.

All, I thought, because of a worm. I suppose deep down I knew it was a bit more than that, because I tried to tell one of the teachers what happened but she said I wasn't to worry about it. That the police would take of things now. And then she turned back and looked at where they were holding Worm Man and said, more to herself than to me, how she'd always known something like this was going to happen.

When we got back to class Mrs. Grant told us that Worm Man - she didn't actually call him that, she just called him the man - wasn't all there and didn't always know what he was doing, but that what he'd tried to do to Denise Aubain was very bad and that no matter how slow a person was, behaviour like that could not be tolerated. She said there were a lot of people like him but that they lived mostly in big cities which were very dangerous places for young people like us, and that even though we lived in a small town we should always be careful with people we didn't know.

We all sat there and listened to her and to the sirens of the police car and then the ambulance as it arrived. And then someone asked if Denise would be all right as if they hadn't just seen the whole thing and didn't remember that it had only been a worm that had fallen down her dress. But then no one seemed to remember except me.

And I started to try and say something and to tell Mrs. Grant what had really happened but it didn't come out right and then she told me just to leave things alone and everything would be taken care of. I could feel tears coming to my eyes, and I knew it was pointless to go on but I did, and she got sort of mad at me, but in a nice way because I think she could see I was about to cry. And then she told us to get out our math books and to turn to page seventy-three, but I couldn't because I couldn't see the page numbers through my tears and Mrs. Grant came and touched me on the shoulder and told me everything would be just fine, that Denise would be just fine. I wanted to tell her that's not why I was crying, but I knew there was no point.

You can never tell adults things they don't want to hear.

The Apparel of Innocence

Friday afternoon and the logging trucks were blowing by without apology, monster wheels hurling sheets of oiled water over Jason's soaked and soiled shape. He peered up from his bike in that fraction of a second before the liquid wall rose from the pavement and saw the drivers hunched forward high in their cabs, wiping at condensation on the interior of their windshields while large wipers slapped at the rain that fell. He cursed each time because he knew they saw him but didn't care. It was pay-day and once they dropped their loads it was off to the bar with no wife and no kids. Just them and the boys and their beer.

Jason stopped pedalling and pulled on his brakes. Swung his leg over the seat and looked behind where the road just ridden disappeared between unscathed forests. Ahead to either side lay obscene tracts of land desecrated by chainsaws and bulldozers.

There was nothing else except the light fog that accompanies rain when the earth is still hoarding its summer heat against the approach of winter. A grey mist viewed through thin, shearing lines of rain that formed a transparent screen.

It had rained for three days, since Jason hit the Washington coast. He'd thought of phoning Susan in Vancouver, of asking her to pick him up. Imagined her doing so and the two of them making up on the way home. Whatever it was he'd done, whatever it was she didn't like, he could change. This whole thing - it was just a phase she was going through.

Take a train, she'd have told him. And stop calling me.

Maybe he had overdone it with the phoning. With the accusations. Sitting in the basement of his parent's house, maybe he'd gone a bit over the edge. Who could blame him? They'd lived together for almost three years. What seemed the whole of his adult life.

Jason thought back two months. Leaving the sunshine and entering the shadows of their one-bedroom apartment. Susan seated at the kitchen table. We need to talk.

She offered him a coffee, then said, You have to move out. No, it's not another man. It's Angelina. No, she didn't know when she first realised. She guessed she'd always known. And no, it was not simply an experimental stage she was going through. Please don't make this any more difficult than it already is.

Christ, Jason said. I'm supposed to make it easy for you? Three fucking years for you to tell me something you've always known, and I'm supposed to make it easy?

She didn't expect him to understand, thank god for that. But she wanted him to know she did love him, just not in the way he wanted. She never would.

So they'd been living one gigantic lie which only she knew, he said. That was great. Just fucking great.

Susan hoped he could one day forgive her.

Two weeks later, he heard Angelina had moved in.

Jason held his bike in one hand and warmed his numb cock with the other. Aimed high and watched the steam rise from the arc of his piss, swearing as the last bit splashed in the mud, over his shoe and onto his bare leg. Tucked his cock away and stuck his leg out from beneath his cape into the rain to wash off the dribble.

He reached under the bungee cord that held his tent and sleeping bag and found the bottle of cheap California red he'd bought in a town whose name he'd already forgotten. But not the old woman who worked the cash in the liquor store. Who wouldn't sell to him without a picture ID. He called her a dried up, toothless bitch and stormed out. Then stopped at the first convenience store.

He felt badly about it now. She was old enough to have been his grandmother. He told himself it wasn't really his fault. It was the rain and the cold and just not his fault. At least he'd given her something to talk about. Jason smiled picturing the old woman telling her story to a shocked family at the dinner table.

He popped the cork with his knife and took three long pulls from the bottle. Thought about rolling a joint, but how could he in this rain?

Tires squelching in the dirt at the side of the road behind startled him. He spun, prepared to leap for the ditch.

The pickup was old. Colour somewhere in the nether land between dark grey and brown. Perfect camouflage for a late September drizzle. He couldn't make out the driver, but the passenger window rolled down and a shout asked where he was headed. Told him to hop in.

Jason threw his bike in the box and climbed into cab.

The driver wore a torn fedora Harpo Marx style - the front lip turned up. Straggly brown hair escaped from beneath, framing an unshaven, grinning face. The driver's name was Captain Crunch. He'd been a real captain. U.S. army. Flew helicopters for a year and a half in 'Nam. Since the war the Captain had been working a saw mill next town over. He accepted a slug of the wine. Jesus, he said. Where'd ya get that shit? Wanna beer? Pulled a six pack from beneath his seat. What're ya going to Castle Creek for? Ain't nothing there.

Need a laundromat, Jason said. Dry out my stuff. Sleeping bag's soaking.

Shit, said the Captain. You're coming home with me. We got

lots a room.

****

Duke and Donnie, the Captain's roommates, were sitting on an old couch that reminded Jason of student furniture. Dark green, stained. Thin cushions and a wooden frame. Their friend, TJ, was in a matching arm chair. The only girl, Traci, sat silently in a kitchen chair. Thick lines of blue eyeshadow, a shade that had been popular about a decade earlier, ran above and below each eye, as though she'd had seen it in an old Cosmopolitan but hadn't quite got it right. On her left ring finger she wore a tiny diamond. She clearly belonged to Donnie.

In the middle of the room sat a battered coffee table littered with beer bottles and overflowing ashtrays. There wasn't much on the walls. One torn poster of a woman with enormous breasts peeking out from beneath a cut off t-shirt. She was holding a can of local brew. A confederate flag, faded by sunshine, served as a partial curtain for the small picture window. Through the doorway behind Traci, Jason was surprised to see the kitchen was fairly clean.

The guys all seemed to work in the same mill. Traci was still in high school and for the most part, they ignored her. Smoked joints and drank no name beer and muscatel. A dollar seventy-five for two quarts, they said. That California shit ain't worth the money. Jason smiled, stuck to beer.

They argued over whose mill crew was the best. Took a manly pride in their production. Told Jason stories of drinking and fighting. Usually with guys from the next town. Usually over football games. Large rumbles in the parking lots. TJ had been a high school football star and the others listened with respect when he spoke. Told stories of his glory days while he waved off their admiration with a sweep of his hand.

Long time ago, he said. Only hoped his son could follow in his footsteps.

Talk moved to the big game the next day. The Belam Panthers and the Castle Creek Spartans - an age old rivalry. Predictions of a slaughter sliced through the smoke. Names of current stars and comparisons with past ones.

Traci sat quietly and watched the newcomer. Donnie was on his feet re-enacting a game-saving touchdown, the others hooting and hollering encouragement. Jason tried to look interested, even tried to join in, but was uncomfortably aware of the girl's stares. Felt his own eyes drawn to her. Noted her small breasts shrink-wrapped in a white t-shirt. Wondered how long she'd been fucking. How long before she'd have a baby and be left at home with the other wives.

In reply to his questions they told Jason education in Belam ended at sixteen, maybe seventeen. Saw mills for the boys. Babies for the girls. They spoke of one who'd almost escaped. His coach convinced him to finish school. Promise of a scholarship. Maybe a shot at the big leagues. If not the NFL, maybe up north, in Canada, which was where he went after two years of college.

Maybe Jason had heard of him. Played for a team that started with an "S."

Probably Saskatchewan, Jason said. The Rough Riders. But no. He'd never heard the name. He didn't tell them he knew none of the players.

No big deal, they said. Got cut his first season. He's a supervisor at one of the mills now. Came back and married his high school sweetheart. They had a baby five months after the wedding, eight months after he returned from Canada without seeing the playing field except from the bench. They all knew whose baby it was.

They told Jason he was bound to meet him. Had a girlfriend in Castle Creek where he went straight from work on Fridays. Then, after he fucked her, he joined the boys. Told stories of his days in professional football. But Jason sensed he didn't get the same respect as TJ. Instead of being the guy who'd played college ball, he was the guy who'd failed to make the pro's.

****

Pit bulls have been given a bad rap, Duke told Jason. These guys are as sweet as could be. Aren't they, Traci? Traci smiled.

The rain had stopped and they were outside behind the house. Had released the dogs from their kennel for a run. The dogs darted away, nipping at each other's hind legs, and then raced to be the first to reach Duke when he called. Smartest dogs I've ever seen, Duke said.

Duke wasn't from Belam. L.A. born and bred, he said. Same as the Captain. But couldn't live there anymore. Too many damned people. Too much trouble.

He and the Captain had been in 'Nam together. Now he felt a sort of responsibility for the Captain. Best chopper pilot there. Saved our asses every goddamn time we went out. Could spot trouble a mile away. The place fucked him up pretty bad, though.

Duke, Jason discovered, didn't work in the mills. Couldn't. Shrapnel in his back and a metal plate in his head had seen to that. Friendly fire, he said with a laugh. Who the fuck ever heard of friendly fire? He wanted to be a writer, wanted to write about the war, but couldn't seem to keep the thing he was trying to say straight in his head. I don't blame anyone, he said. What would be the point?

One of the dogs was trying to hump the other and Duke yelled at them. Stupid bastards. They're both goddamn males. Traci giggled.

The others had left on a beer run, which meant they'd stop at The Belam Hotel. Only bar in town. Depending on who was there, they could be gone an hour or all night. Duke wanted to shower before they got back.

I was working in the garden. Down by the creek. Got some

great plants growing, he told Jason. Told Traci to show him while he was inside.

Traci smiled shyly. Asked if Jason wanted to see and they headed down the muddy embankment. The dogs, sensing the opportunity for a walk, raced down the path ahead of them.

Don't let them get too far, Duke shouted. They aren't that smart.

They stood by the stream, Jason asking Traci about school to break the awkward silence. She gave one word answers, unused to the attention of a stranger, a foreigner. When he asked about the ring, she looked away for the dogs, called for them to come closer. The dogs looked and wagged their tails but made no move toward them.

His plants are over here, she said. Led him down a path that ran next to the stream. She stopped surrounded by a dozen or so six-foot plants. They're his pride and joy. He takes really good care of them.

They look great, Jason said. That what we're smoking?

Yeah. She led him further along the path. You go to college? she asked.

Yes.

Your girlfriend?

Yes.

What's her name?

Susan.

What's she doing now?

Jason lied. Fucking some guy we went to school with. Then he apologised. I shouldn't have said that.

Why not?

I don't know. She was just a bit messed up. Didn't know what she wanted. The kind of person who thinks the grass is always greener on the other side of the fence. Anyway, nothing I can do about it now. We broke up a little while ago. Just before I left. They watched the dogs. You going to marry Donnie?

I suppose so.

Why? He meant because she was so young.

What else am I gonna do?

****

New faces arrived with the others from The Belam. To see the Canadian. Big guy named Bear took a liking to Jason. Sat on the floor beside him and gave him periodic one-armed hugs. Shit, he kept saying. Canada, eh? and then laughed.

They continued telling Jason drinking stories, each man shouting contributions. They all knew every story. Were all there for each and every one.

Then someone shouted for TJ to get his guitar out of his truck. He told them, they want him to play, someone else had to go get it. When it arrived, he brought out a stool. Asked what they wanted to hear.

My Daddy Died Young, everyone shouted. Told Jason how it was his own song. How he wrote the whole thing himself.

And for a moment there was silence except for the guitar and TJ. Then applause and shouts for TJ to play it again. He did and then leaned his guitar carefully against the wall. Asked who the fuck stole his beer.

When Jason went to the kitchen to get more beer, Traci followed. Fussed idly with something on the counter.

What's it like where you're from, she wanted to know.

Much the same, he told her. Lots of trees.

I mean the guys. Do they sit around every weekend smoking and drinking?

Sometimes, Jason said. We go out for dinners a lot. Usually there's more women.

In the living room they were making plans for revenge. Some asshole in a blue pickup smashed Donnie's truck while we were drinking at the Belam last Saturday, they told Jason. We see him, he's a dead man.

Donnie loved his truck. Grabbed Jason and dragged him outside to see it. Fire-engine red short box with chrome exhausts climbing either side of the cab. Chrome runners and mags. Bumper sticker read Truckers Haul Ass and had a small cartoon of five bare-bottomed women in the back of a pickup. Donnie showed him where the blue truck hit his front wheel well. Gonna cost me five hundred bucks easy to fix.

They entered the house where a decision was being made. Did they beat the shit out of the guy, or just take baseball bats to his truck? Wanted to know what Donnie wants to do. After all, it was his truck.

Jason could feel the effects of the beer and the pot. Felt himself sliding into their mode. Like a chameleon. Listened to himself saying, Let's kill the fucker. Realised he'd surprised no one but himself. No one knew him and he could say anything. The realisation made him smile.

****

They were playing pool under the smoky lights at The Belam. Country music wailing from old speakers suspended from the four corners of the bar. Paraphernalia from the fifties that most city bars would kill for covered the walls and a high shelf that ran around the room.

A dozen or so draft glasses, most now empty, covered one tabletop next to them. Another held empty shot glasses. Bear hollered to the waitress to bring another round.

Hold on to your shorts, she yelled back. Bear told her he'd rather she held on to what was in his shorts.

They went outside to smoke a joint in the parking lot. Stood beside one of the trucks and talked about who had the best shit and who was fucking who. Said "Eh" and laughed because Jason was Canadian.

Back inside, Jason stood at the bar alone to catch his breath, to get reoriented. A woman old enough to be his mother approached, cornered him. Rubbed her iron encased breasts against his arm. Seemed oblivious to the bulge of her stomach that stretched her tights to their limit. Leaned in close so her smoky gin breath was hot in his face and talked about sex. Oral sex is great, she said, but there's nothing like coming with a good stiff cock inside you. Which do you like better?

Jason made an awkward joke about never having had the second.

Eleanor flashed a brief smirk, as though she wasn't really listening. Never had a Canadian, she said. Her hand grazed across the zipper of his jeans. I exercise my cunt muscles, she told him. Could grip you so tight you'd be crying for mercy.

That right? Jason said. He looked to Traci for help. Slipped by Eleanor when she turned to see who he was looking at. Heard her call Traci a little slut under her breath. Or maybe she'd meant him.

Jason started playing pool with Donnie, cigarette dangling from his mouth when he shot. Did another shooter of Jack Daniels that Bear handed him. Could barely see the cue ball let alone hit it.

The Captain wanted to play and Jason handed him his cue, let him take his turn. Bear looked at him with drunken affection. You're okay, he said. Gave him one of his bear hugs and said, I'm gonna buy you a beer.

Jesus Christ, Bear, TJ sneered. You gonna be sucking his dick by the end of the night.

You calling me a fag? Everyone froze as Bear moved towards TJ. You calling me a fag?

TJ knew he'd made a mistake. Tried to laugh. Naw, Bear. Just joking, man.

Bear stood glaring. Then the muscles in his neck relaxed. You damn right you just joking. 'Cause if you ain't, I gotta kill ya. Then he laughed, too.

You have to be careful how you deal with these guys, Duke said quietly to Jason. I don't know how things are in Canada, but you have to be careful how you deal with these guys.

Suddenly, Donnie bolted for the door yelling something Jason didn't hear. Bear and TJ ran out after him. Jason looked to Traci and held up his hands asking what was up.

Traci shrugged. Who knows? Same old shit I expect. Someone Donnie wants to fight must've walked in.

They watched the door, but only TJ reappeared.

Where's Donnie? Traci asked.

It was the guy with the blue pickup. Donnie and Bear took off after him.

Traci turned back to Jason. It's like this every weekend. Every goddamn weekend. Sixteen, and this is what I have to look forward to. Have a kid and I won't even have this.

It doesn't have to be like this, Jason said.

No? Who you think's gonna change it?

****

Jason was drinking with conviction. A man who'd made a decision. He was going to change it. Going to save Traci. Didn't know how. Only knew that what he saw was wrong and he was the only one who could - who would - do anything about it.

He'd made his decision in the bar, after Donnie and Bear returned. Donnie'd been such an asshole, hopping around telling everyone about tearing down the road after the guy. How he was so fucking lucky they didn't catch him. Like it took some kind of brains to put a foot on the accelerator. Christ, they never even saw the guy again. When Traci had tried to calm Donnie, he'd pushed her away roughly.

And now, watching Traci in the living room, Jason recognised the beauty of her simplicity, of her naiveté. Realised how different she was from Susan.

She needed someone. Of this he was convinced. She needed someone like him.

With each beer and each joint, his conviction grew stronger. But how would he save her? Pay her way to college? Marry her? He had no money. But marriage? That was a possibility. She was pretty. She could go to school and learn things. He could teach her things himself. Hadn't he just finished his Masters?

He stood, intending to approach her, intending to tell her he was going to take her away from all of this. The room tilted, and he tumbled. Landed hard on his side. From the floor, he could see them laughing. Even Traci, the one he was to rescue. His only beloved.

Bear pulled him to a sitting position. Jason did his rag doll imitation. Tried to stand on rubber knees. Heard someone telling him to stay put.

Can't, he managed to utter. Gotta puke. Quick shouts and hands lifted him by the armpits and dragged him - no - hurled him toward the door. And then he was on his knees spewing out liquid. I didn't have anything to eat, he mumbled. Someone was holding his head up by his hair. If this guy lets go, Jason thought, I'm face first in it.

He tried to shuffle his knees forward, so they'd be beneath him. Didn't feel gravel digging into his knees and hoped he was on wood. Remembered there was no porch and figured he'd deal with his knees in the morning. Knew he had to get up, but couldn't.

When it was clear he was through puking, they hauled him back over his legs and propped him against the wall. Sit here a bit, someone told him. Get some air.

Someone else said, I'm going in, and Jason saw by the size it was Bear. Tried to thank him, but by the time the words came out the screen door had swung shut.

Duke slid down beside him. Don't worry about any of this, he said. Usually these guys would've beaten you to it.

He okay? The Captain had come out to check on him. Squatted beside Duke.

Yeah, he's okay.

Jason tried to look at them and smile, to show that he understood and still had a sense of humour about it all and that really he was a good guy who just didn't realise he'd had so much, but his head rolled loose and out of control on his neck.

****

Jason awoke in darkness, his head pounding. He knew he was in a bed. He also knew someone had their mouth on his cock. At first his only thought was amazement that he was able to get an erection. He tried to rise, to see who was sucking on him, but a hand pushed him back down.

Relax, a voice told him.

The voice. He knew the voice. He struggled to lift himself, tried to push the head off his cock, but the hand on his chest kept him down and the head bobbed between his legs. Jason sank back into the bed. No. Don't. He wasn't even sure if he'd spoken the words aloud. The mouth slid up and down and he felt the pressure build.

He tried to imagine it was Susan between his legs. No. Not Susan. Traci. He pictured Traci in his mind. The way she'd looked playing pool. Her body snug in her t-shirt and jeans. Jason gripped the sheets tightly and thrust his hips upward as he erupted into Duke's mouth.

****

The next morning Bear brought his two sons to the house. They were supposed to be going fishing.

Later, he told them. Get outside and play with the dogs.

But it's raining! they complained.

Hardly enough to wet a virgin, he told them. Now git before I whop your backsides. They left with heads hung low as their father took a joint from the Captain.

'Bout time you got up, the Captain told Jason. They hadn't been to bed yet. Had gone back to The Belam and closed the place around four. Then home, drinking and smoking and playing music.

I put your stuff in the dryer, Duke told him.

Jason made no response. His head still pounded and he tried not to think of the night before. He wondered if there was anything to eat. Went to the kitchen where Traci was making toast and frying sausages. Through her light cotton dress Jason could see the outline of her bra and panties. The shape of her legs. His groin stirred and he thought of her sucking him the night before. Shook himself as he remembered it hadn't been her. Not really. Only in his mind. Returned her smile awkwardly and returned to the safety of the living room. Accepted the joint offered to him. Avoided looking at Duke.

Did you find the blue pickup? he asked.

No, but they didn't look disappointed. It left them something to look forward to.

You gotta come with us today, Donnie told him. Gonna be a great ball game. Then he yelled into the kitchen for food. Christ, he said. What the fuck is taking her so long? And bring us all another beer.

Jason rose to get the beer, but Donnie told him to sit. She'll do it, he said.

You know these guys was in 'Nam? Bear asked. Killed fucking people. Go on, Captain. Tell him about it. He's Canadian. He probably don't know shit about it.

Naw, said the Captain. Fuck that shit.

Fuck that shit nothing. Tell him a goddamn story.

I said I don't want to.

Bear turned to Jason. One time these guys wasted a sniper from their chopper just as they were landing. Turned out to be a fucking girl. Only she wasn't dead. So one of the guys - what was his name, Captain?

Fuck you, the Captain said, and stomped out of the room.

Bear turned to Duke. You was there. What the fuck was that guy's name that did her?

Sometimes you're such a fucking asshole, Duke said and followed the Captain.

What? What the fuck did I do?

Shut the fuck up, TJ said.

You shut the fuck up. Bear turned to Jason. You wanna hear the rest of the story or what?

Not really.

Ah, fuck y'all anyway. Grabbed a beer from Traci's hand. Turned back to Jason. You ever kill anyone?

****

Jason rode with Donnie to the game, Traci sandwiched between them. I hear you got ditched back home, Donnie said, between pulls on his beer.

Jason felt Traci tense. He gave a small laugh. Guess you could say that.

Women are bitches. Ain't that right, Traci. All except you, of course.

Traci smiled weakly.

Of course, takes a real asshole to steal a friend's girl. Another beer? Give him a beer, Traci.

There was no sign of the blue pickup in the parking lot. In the stands, they drank beer from smuggled cans through straws. Donnie sat at the end of the bench opposite Jason, his one arm around Traci, his other alternating between flicking his cigarette and directing a straw into his mouth. He asked how Jason was enjoying the game. A real shit kicker, ain't it? The score was not even close. Short of a real fuck up, the Panthers would go home victorious.

Donnie began talking about killing the bastard with the blue pickup again. He was looking around the bleachers. Caught Traci and Jason exchanging glances. Jason saw his lip tighten. Turned and asked the Captain if he was heading back to the house.

What d'ya mean the house? Donnie yelled. No one's going back to the house. We gonna have us some fun.

****

After the game Duke, Traci and Jason went home while the others went to the Belam or to look for the blue pickup. Jason wasn't sure. Once home, they smoked a joint, and then Traci suggested they take the dogs for a walk. Duke stayed behind to rest.

They walked through the woods in silence until Traci turned to Jason. Do you think I'm pretty?

Very.

And his girlfriend?

His ex-girlfriend. What about her?

Is she pretty?

Yes.

Prettier than her?

Different.

Is that why you always watch me?

Jason responded by kissing her. He groped at her breasts, squeezing them firmly. Lifted her dress and rubbed his hand hard against her mound. Then pushed her panties to her knees. Traci stepped back and slipped off her sandals. Stepped out of her panties while Jason undid his pants. They fell to the pathway, still damp from the previous day’s rain, and made love. Jason was aware that he was hurried and rough with her.

Afterward, they sat, his back to a tree, her back to his. Sometimes I want to leave here, she said, but there's nowhere to go. No way to get there even if there was.

What about college?

No money. Besides, her father would never send her. Women don't need to be educated.

Jason thought about his decision the night before. About his decision to rescue her. We should go soon, he said.

Shit! Traci leaped to her feet. Goddamn Shit!

What?

You bruised me. She showed him her thighs. I've got goddamn bruises! What the hell am I gonna say if Donnie sees?

Tell him he did it. He won't know the difference. For all Jason knew, Donnie had bruised her.

****

At the house there was no sign of Duke, and they showered quickly. The others returned as Jason was coming out of his room, towelling his hair.

Where's the hell's Traci? Donnie demanded.

I don't know. In your room I suppose. He used the towel to hide his face.

Traci! Donnie's eyes remained on Jason as he yelled.

Traci came out wearing jeans and a sweatshirt, her hair still damp.

You fucker! Donnie lunged at Jason. For a moment they were locked together, then several bodies pulled them apart.

Traci screamed at them to stop. Nothing happened, she was telling Donnie.

All right, all right! Donnie shook Bear's hands off him. Then what the hell are you two showering for?

We were just walking the dogs, for Christ's sake. In case you haven't noticed, it's been raining for three days. Do you have any idea how muddy it is out there?

Come on, Donnie. Don't be an asshole.

Donnie glared at Jason. Don't think I haven't noticed you looking at her. Jason said nothing. Donnie turned to Traci. You better be telling the fucking truth or I'll kill you. You ever fuck around on me ...

Jesus Christ, the Captain said. This is fucking ridiculous. It's the middle of the fucking afternoon, for Christ's sake.

What the fuck's that gotta do with anything?

Christ, gimmie a beer.

What‘s going on? Duke had come out of his room.

Nothing. Donnie shouted. Nothing's going on. You been here all along?

Yeah. Why?

Nothing. Who's gotta joint?

****

The Belam was full of people who'd been to the game celebrating their team's win.

Outside, someone passed Jason a joint.

Donnie watched him toke and asked if he was gonna puke again. You should have seen him, he told the others. Couldn't fucking stand up. Puking like a fucking dog in the lane.

Traci told him to stop. Instead, Donnie imitated Jason falling on his face in the living room, lying on the carpet pleading he's about to puke. Guess they never taught you how to drink up there in Canada, he said.

Jason took the joint from his mouth. Guess not.

Bear held out a plastic bag. Time for ‘shrooms.

The foul taste in his mouth raised a familiar wave of nausea, and Jason washed the mushrooms down quickly with beer.

Forty-five minutes later Jason realised he was pretty high. Sat at a corner table chain-smoking and chugging beer like water. The Captain joined him for a few minutes to make sure he was all right and then returned to the boisterous action around the pool table. Jason was drifting with his thoughts when he looked up and found Eleanor seated beside him.

Paranoia of acting too high made Jason overly polite. She asked if he wanted to go outside for a joint.

Darkness had fallen. They sat in the front seat of her old Buick and passed the joint between them while Eleanor talked non-stop. As Jason watched her smoke, his eyes drifted to her breasts which hung large and loose beneath her cotton shirt. He reached over and fondled one. Eleanor gasped and her eyes fluttered. Surprised by the depth of her response, Jason undid the top two buttons of her shirt and fondled her nipples, curious to see how erect they would become. Felt like he was playing doctor. Was acutely aware of her breathing becoming deeper. He squeezed roughly, watched her wince. Removed his hand and told her to pull down her jeans. Watched without emotion as she slid the car seat back as far as possible and then struggled to free her expanding flesh of the self-imposed constraint.

Jason tugged his own pants down, kicked one ankle free. Their hands found each others groins. And then Eleanor was on her back, Jason pumping furiously between her legs. As he pushed she slid so that her head fell below the steering wheel. Ow, she cried. Take it easy.

But an anger gripped Jason's body and he pushed harder with each thrust. Felt a hatred for the woman below him. Wished he could reach through the wheel and smash the face that was telling him to stop. Allowed himself to be content with the sight of her head being scrunched against the door.

Suddenly Eleanor's muscles constricted and Jason’s cock was being crushed in a vise. He screamed, she let go, and he withdrew. Jesus Christ, he said. What the fuck?

He pulled up his pants as she pulled herself out from beneath the steering wheel. What the fuck? she mimicked. What the fuck's your problem. Called him a fucking bastard as he left the car without a word.

Traci looked up when him came through the door of the bar. Turned away quickly. The guys were laughing.

Fuck you all, ran through Jason's mind as he pulled out a stool. He watched Eleanor return and walk to the opposite end of the bar.

He thought about what had happened outside. It wasn't that bad. He was just too high. The tension that had run through his body hadn't been anger so much as it had been adrenaline. He’d just been a little over zealous. Over energetic. She'd been the one who'd been out of line. She'd invited him out there. Hadn't she told him just the day before that she liked a good fuck more than almost anything? So what changed?

But he didn't blame her. The whole thing had been a simple misunderstanding caused by drugs - nothing new. He hadn't wanted to be with her in the first place. Had only been because he was high and didn't know how to say no.

He would simply explain this to her. But as he approached, she turned and told him to go back to his fucking igloo. He moved away shaking his head. She was obviously too stupid to understand.

****

They’d given up their search and were on a dirt road headed home when their headlights swung onto the blue pickup. The driver was standing by the back bumper taking a piss. Donnie swerved in beside him. Before the driver knew what was happening, Bear and Donnie hopped out and stood between him and his cab. Jason stayed in Donnie’s truck, one foot out on the runner.

Well, well, well. Looky what we got here, Bear. I do believe we been looking for you.

The driver looked nervous. Hey, guys. What's up? His speech was slightly slurred.

Donnie mimicked him. Wash up, Bear? Wash up? Well, you stupid fuck head. I'll tell you what's up. You been a little careless with your driving. That's what's up.

The driver was trying to zip his fly when Donnie gave him a shove. He stumbled back. Hey. What the fuck you doing?

Well, you little shit. This is what I'm doing. Donnie shoved him again. This time the driver was ready. He grabbed Donnie's arm with one hand and with the other delivered a blow to Donnie's head. Bear was on him immediately, pinning his arms behind.

You gonna regret that, you stupid shit. Keep him still, Bear.

The driver struggled, began to protest, but Donnie knocked the wind out of him with his first punch. What's that you were gonna say? Donnie brought his fist down on the driver's neck. Then raised his knee hard up into his face. The driver sagged in Bear's arms.

Donnie glared down at him. You wanted to say something? Then he turned to Jason. Get out here, man. You don't wanna miss all the fun.

I'm okay.

I said get the fuck out here! Then he swung his left fist up into the driver's face.

Jason jumped from the cab and grabbed Donnie's arm. For Christ's sake. Don't kill him.

Donnie shook free of his hand. Why not? He's just a useless piece of shit anyway. Ain't that right, Bear. Fuck with another man's truck. Kinda makes him a useless piece of shit, wouldn't you say? Donnie smiled at Jason.

Jesus, man. It's only a dent.

It's the principle, man. It's the principle. You got principles, don’t you, Jason? Well, this guy don't. Fact, he's kinda like that guy that's fucking your girlfriend. Probably sticking it to her right now. Now, there's a guy with no principles. I bet that were him Bear was holding, you wouldn't have no problem with this. Go on. He waved his arm toward the driver.

Fuck you, Jason said. Leave the guy alone. He turned to Bear. For Christ's sake, Bear.

Bear let go and looked at the lump on the road. He's right, Donnie. Let's get outa here.

All right, Donnie replied. Fuck you both. Took one last kick at the driver's stomach.

One hundred yards away Donnie swung his truck around. What are you doing? Jason demanded.

Relax. Just gonna have a little fun.

In the headlights they could see the driver kneeling by his truck. When he saw their approach he lurched toward his door. Yanked it open. But as Donnie made his pass close to the door, instead of leaping into the front seat, the driver's body tottered gruesomely backward. They heard the crunch of his head against the front top corner of Donnie's truck. His body rose, hung for one interminable second before them, and then bounced off the windshield.

They all began shouting at once. Fuck. You killed the fucker. Jesus Christ. Stop the truck. They slid to a halt.

Shit. Donnie said. Shit, shit, shit.

The body had been thrown into the ditch. Even in the darkness they could see there was no use checking for life. The head had been smashed open. Brain matter hung like a wet rag over his forehead and ran down what was left of his face.

Shit. Fucking shit, Jason kept repeating. What the fuck have you done?

Shut the fuck up, Donnie told him. Shit. I was only trying to scare him. Fucking shit. What the fuck was he doing?

They sat by the side of the road peering down into the ditch. What the fuck are we going to do?

What do you mean, what the fuck are we going to do? We've got to report this, Jason said.

Right. That's fucking brilliant, asshole. And all three of us will end up in the slammer.

We could say it was an accident. That we were just driving along when this drunk opened his door and came tumbling out into our path.

Oh, please. Nobody's gonna believe that. We beat the shit out of him first.

But he could have got that when we hit him.

Donnie stood. No way, he shouted. We're not telling anyone. They got ways of telling where injuries come from you know. Don't you ever watch fucking television. Now shut the fuck up while I think.

He's right, Bear said. We gotta do something else.

Are you both fucking nuts? You're talking about murder.

That's already been done. We're talking about how to fucking hide it.

Walker's Falls. Donnie said. Walker's Falls! That's it. That's our answer.

What the fuck are you talking about?

It's about six miles from here, Bear said. Runs into a gorge. They say its real deep. Bodies that go in there can stay forever.

We can drive his truck there and dump the body, Donnie said. Leave a bottle. They'll think he got drunk and fell.

If you can believe what you hear, it won't be the first time. And there's no way to prove any different. Divers can't go in 'cause of the falls.

I can't believe what you're talking about, Jason said. For Christ's sake, we can't just ...

We can and we will. And you're gonna keep your fucking mouth shut. You're in this as much as we are.

I didn't do anything!

Let me put it this way, Donnie said. You're gonna keep your fucking mouth shut unless you want to end up in Walker's Falls with this asshole.

I can't believe what the fuck we're about to do.

Believe it, man, Bear said. Don't worry. We got it all worked out.

It took the three of them to lift the body from the ditch and place it in the bed of Donnie's truck. They could wash it out later. They went back with a flashlight looking for parts they may have missed. Buried the small pieces of blood and brains and covered up the area with brush and leaves.

Wearing gloves they found in the cab, Bear drove the blue pickup.

At the top of the falls they filled the body's pockets with rocks. Tied a heavy towing chain from Donnie's truck box around its waist. Jason watched as Bear and Donnie counted one - two - three and hurled the body out from the cliff, like some macabre birthday rite. It tumbled slowly, then disappeared in a wash of foam.

We can't leave the truck here, said Donnie.

Why the fuck not?

What if they drag? What if they find him?

Ain't no way that gonna happen.

But what if? Why the fuck not just move the truck so they don't look here?

What the fuck do we do with it?

We move it a couple of miles. Then you jump from it into mine and we keep on moving. That way - no fucking tracks, no fucking way to link it to us.

Do that, Jason said, and they're going to know something's wrong. Remember, you want them to think he's in the falls.

Right, Donnie said. He wore the hint of a smile.

****

Dawn was breaking as Jason wheeled his bicycle from the shed, rode down the lane and turned west onto the country highway. He pushed down hard on the pedals, cycled without looking back. The sun rose above the trees behind him but despite its increasing warmth, Jason shivered.

He passed the turnoff for Castle Creek before his legs slowed their gruelling pace. He was suddenly aware of his heart pumping hard and fast. Of his blood coursing through his veins, pounding in his temples, throbbing just beneath the surface of his skin as though seeking to escape from its confines, threatening to pop his eyeballs out of their sockets. No part of him wanted to be there. He wished he could disintegrate and start again.

He heard a vehicle overtaking him, but paid no attention. And then it was cutting in front of him, swinging onto the dirt shoulder, blocking his path with a cloud of metal and dust. Jason skidded to a halt as Bear and Donnie leaped out.

They wanted to know what he was doing taking off without saying goodbye. Without allowing them to send him off properly. Wanted to know where he was headed in such a rush. You wouldn't be planning on telling anyone about what happened now, would you?

If I was going to, I'd have stopped in Castle Creek. I wouldn't be out here.

Because you know, you're in this as much as either of us, Donnie said. He peered straight into Jason's eyes. Tried to read what lay beneath the surface. Could he trust Jason to keep his mouth shut? You know it was an accident. You do realise that, don't you? No one wanted what happened to happen. You got remember that. It was simply an accident. We weren't going anywhere near him, but the asshole was drunk. He fell in front of us. We didn't drive into him. You got remember that. Now he's dead. It was an accident. And there ain't nothing we can do about it. But there ain't no use in anyone getting into trouble over an accident. It ain't gonna bring him back, and it ain't gonna do you or me or Bear any good us telling people what happened. You understand? You do understand that, Jason.

It was a statement, not a question.

Jason nodded. Looked from Donnie to Bear who was leaning against the truck listening. I just want to get out of here, Jason finally said. Just leave. I don't know anything about anything.

That's right, said Donnie. Nothing 'bout nothing. Ain't that right, Bear, he said over his shoulder, his eyes remaining on Jason. We know nothing 'bout nothing.

That's right, Bear said softly. Nothing 'bout nothing.

Had it been any other time, the repetition might have made Jason laugh. Like a hypnosis scene in a very bad movie. But he felt numb and helpless. And stupid. And maybe that's what he wanted them to do. Hypnotise him so he could remember nothing of the past forty-eight hours. So there would be no Captain, no Duke, and no Traci. No body churning silent and endless, flushing away piece by piece in its liquid casket. So the town of Belam would remain hidden from him for the rest of his life. So he could continue living.

Besides, Donnie said. There might be some difference between your story and ours. Makes you wonder, came down to that, who the fuck they'd believe? Two local boys or a single foreigner passing through. Especially - Donnie nodded his head slowly as a thought occurred to him - especially after so many people heard you say we should kill the fucker.

It won't come down to that.

No. Don't suppose it will.

****

Jason reached the coast and turned south on 101. Each time a car approached, his legs stopped pumping while his heart did double time. He stared straight ahead, certain that guilt howled from his face. Only one police car passed. Afterward, Jason got off his bike. Coughed and spit but managed not to puke.

The first night Jason found a nearly deserted campsite on a ridge above the coast. He set his tent so the opening faced the ocean, then sat inside and watched the sun set. For those five minutes when the sun's disappearance seems to kick into high gear, when the sun seems impatient to be gone after a long day of traversing the sky, Jason was able to forget where he was - who he was.

Then he thought about it. Sure he'd been there when the accident - and it was an accident - had occurred. But he hadn't done anything. Hadn't even wanted to be there in the first place. Had only gone because Donnie had urged him to, probably to keep Jason and Traci apart. Bear had also insisted and no one argued with Bear. Besides, if anything, Jason had stopped the beating, had kept it from being an actual murder.

Now he had no choice but to go along with the cover-up. It was his word against theirs, and everyone knows they never trust strangers in these ass backward little towns. What chance would he have? At the very least, he'd be in the courts for the next year, unable to leave the country, and be found guilty as an accomplice. Worse, he could be found guilty of murder. Donnie and Bear could blame the whole thing on him and he'd go to jail for something he didn't do. He wondered if Washington had the death penalty.

Jason realised he'd followed the only course of action open to him, and he was finally able to close his eyes and sleep.

For the next few days, Jason scoured the papers, half expecting to see an artist's rendition of himself. But there was no mention of a disappearance in Washington. No mention of a police search.

Instead there were stories of a man who'd escaped from the jaws of a great white off the coast of southern Oregon. In the photographs the man proudly displayed fresh teeth marks that ran diagonally across his chest and back.

And there was a story about a man who was riding his bicycle around the states trying to drum up support for his bid to become President. They showed an old man standing beside a bicycle plastered in American flags. He held another in each hand as he smiled his toothless grin for the camera.

But there was no mention of a disappearance, and Jason began to question his memory. Had it even occurred the way he thought it had? He'd been on mushrooms. Maybe he'd hallucinated the whole thing. If not the whole thing, at least part of it. The part that he couldn't bring himself to think of. Otherwise, surely it would be in the papers. Otherwise, surely they'd be looking for him.

Slowly Jason relaxed. Stopped tensing each time a vehicle approached or he walked by a cop in some small coastal town. Stopped leafing through newspapers, searching the headlines of the short pieces that fill out the back pages.

And he changed his campsite just once - in northern California - after a group of guys dropped by with beer to see where he was from.

About the Author

Ronald Sparling grew up in Montreal, Canada, but has lived abroad since 1994, when he first moved to Beijing. Since then, he has lived in eight different countries. Most of his time has been spent as a freelance writer and photographer with his work appearing in publications throughout S.E. Asia and North America. He has also had restaurants in Vietnam and Thailand.

Currently, Sparling lives with his wife in Kuala Lumpur, Malaysia, where he continues to write and shoot while teaching Photography and Communications Technology at Sunway University College.

This is his first book.

www.ingramcontent.com/pod-product-compliance
Lightning Source LLC
Chambersburg PA
CBHW051015060726
47593CB00016B/386

9780995286115